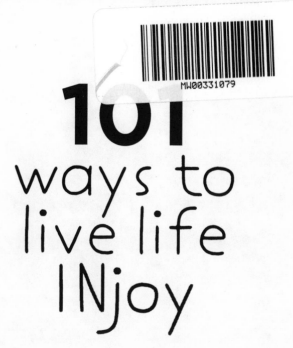

101
ways to live life INjoy

dionne c. monsanto
foreword by **farai chideya**

Printed in New York, NY, USA by Dionne C. Monsanto.

ISBN 978-1-7373903-0-5 (Paperback)
ISBN 978-1-7373903-1-2 (ebook)

Library of Congress Number: 2021911570

DEDICATION

This book is primarily dedicated to Siwe and Agnes, my daughter and mother, as they both gave birth to me. It is also dedicated to my ancestors and the Fastgirls.

A SPECIAL BONUS FROM dionne:
101 Ways to Live Life INjoy Journal

There's so much confusing information out there about how to create a more joy-filled life, especially when we are continuously faced with unexpected challenges and setbacks.

Now that you have your copy of **101 Ways to Live Life INjoy**, you have taken the first step to create your path to joy. You are on your way to connecting to both yourself and others in a spirit of growth, health, and compassion. To help you continue on your way, I created this special bonus to add to your joy toolkit.

The ***101 Ways to Live Life INjoy Journal*** will help you capture your aha moments and reflections from the book, so you can implement them faster and more easily. **#LiveLifeINjoy**

Just go to the link below and tell us where to send it. **JoyousOcean.com/journal**

I'm rooting for you! I look forward to hearing about your breakdowns as well as your breakthroughs!

Here's to living life
INjoy,

Dionne C. Monsanto
Chief Joy Connector
dionne@joyousocean.com

TABLE OF CONTENTS

FOREWORD

Dionne C. Monsanto is a self-made woman in so many ways, including that she re-made her body with yoga, spirit, fire, and willpower; and, as she puts it in the book, knows what it means when a "heart has been cut, bruised, and hopefully sewn back together." She has crafted herself into someone who transmutes pain into progress, and who is constantly aligning herself with her own needs and the needs of the world.

As someone who has just begun to work with Dionne, I see the passion she has for transforming other people's lives as well. Her work INjoy is a practice of community healing, and as a woman of African descent with family in the United States and throughout southern Africa, I love her affirming approach to weaving culture into everything. And while I struggle with re-forming my eating and my body, Dionne's focus on thinking of this as the process of creating my future self, one even more deeply connected to my ancestors and the future I want to leave subsequent generations, has been powerful.

We are living in complex and trying times, when naked political and economic attacks on justice are commonplace and where death has entered too many of our homes during the pandemic. Now is a time of both uncertainty and renewal, and Dionne is here to help us connect to ourselves and each other in a spirit of growth, health, and soul. These chapters give us a chance to receive her wisdom and embody it ourselves.

Farai Chideya
Author and Host/creator, *Our Body Politic*

MEMORIES MAKE ME

I DON'T HAVE A PLAN FOR THE 10TH ANNIVERSARY OF MY DAUGHTER'S DEATH. #fail

I am a planner! I plan what I eat. I plan what I wear. I plan when I get a manicure, when I get a pedicure, when I take a nap, I plan when I'm going to plan. I even make time to plan with friends. "So how could you have forgotten to plan for this?!" I say to myself. I yell at myself.

It is December 2020, and I am gutted that I do not have an idea of how I will celebrate Siwe and the 15 years she lived. I am berating myself and working myself into a full on anxiety attack. "Dionne really? You knew this day was coming? What are you going to do?!" Dionne calm down.

I walk to her bedroom to sit and reflect. It's beautiful here. I love this room; it is so bright and cheery. I'm surrounded by her books and her pictures. Pictures of her with her friends, with me, with her brothers. It holds her guitars, her trophies, her ashes. She is dead. Grief strikes like hot iron and I am gutted and raw AGAIN. I cry. A snot-nosed ugly cry. She has been dead for almost 10 years and you cannot even think of a tribute befitting of her?! I am failing her again. I cry and hold her Elmo and fall asleep crying.

I wake up, light a candle and incense. I sit with Elmo and we stare. We stare at the bottom of her bookshelf at the doors I never open. Those 2 doors protect all of her journals, her writings and the things that weren't published. She was a writer. She did not get to publish her novel or her children's book. She did not get to...

WAIT! That's it! I will write a book! I say I am living the life I never lived AND the life she cannot live, right? So I have to write, I have to publish. So I look at Siwe's picture in front of her ashes and tell her I am going to write a book. Decision. Decided!

The best way for me to honor the 10th anniversary of Siwe's death is for me to write a book.

So many people know me as I am now ASD (after Siwe's death) so they think it was always this way. And others, when they learn of my daughter's death by suicide, or the myriad of deaths and unfortunate situations I have lived through, they marvel at my smile. They ask me how I did it. They call me brave. This book is only the beginning of me detailing the how. I am not done and life will have more tests for me. I know I will keep having opportunities to test my strategies out over and over again.

Being told I am not a good writer, I wrote this book afraid and to prove to myself that I could. I needed to make my inner 5 year old happy and proud.

I wrote and published this book because I could and my deceased daughter, Siwe, could not. In my heart, I wrote this book so others would know that they are not alone. I want my tribe to find me. I need to know I am not alone.

This book is for you if you, like me, are a woman that is all things for so many people and but not for YOU.

If you are feeling alone (maybe even abandoned) as you deal with life's challenges, may this book be a beacon of light for you.

This message is bigger than me and has to be shared. It is my hope that it will impact thousands or millions who are in despair with little or no hope. I hope some-one says, "If she can do it, so can I." In my bones, I know 2 things and they keep me going.

Joy is your birthright.
Transformation is possible.
Live Life INjoy!

To get the most out of this book, read it and read it often. You can read it front to back OR you can pick a number and go there. OR you can use my favorite method! Hold the book to your heart, close your eyes, open the book, and see what message you were meant to receive in that moment. Life does not always have rhyme or reason.

When I was young, I used to write. When I was young, I used to dance. I wrote so freely from my heart with all the emotions of a child unfettered and free. As I got older, I still wrote — but not as freely because my voice had gotten locked away inside. The violation of my unfettered thoughts on paper being read without permission. The violation of being told that if it was written down it was supposed to be read took hold of my writing. So my writing had to go deep within. It lived in my brain. It lived in my heart. It lived in my knees. It lived in my back. It lived in my belly and I gave in to the most precious things being left unsaid.

It lived in my feet, and I danced and I danced and I danced. Some of the things that shouldn't have lived in my body, that should have been on paper got stuck.

Now my writing most freely rolls out of my mouth, into the air taking shape. **WORDS**

Sometimes it rolls and flows throughout my entire body and makes shapes and flies into the air. **DANCE**

Sometimes it flows through my body and takes shape and holds them with breath. **YOGA**

I am my writing.

My life is my book.

1

Participate joyfully in the sorrows of the world. We cannot cure the world of sorrows, but we can choose to live in joy.
— Joseph Campbell

IN JOY. INjoy! Reading the quote above took me down a rabbit hole to find what I had written before. I was giddy and tickled. Writing a book is an unearthing, a birthing and re-birthing of sorts. I wrote the words below as a blog post on October 11, 2010.

It has been a lifelong goal of mine, to be happy.

I recall a friend of mine asking me what I wanted to be when I grew up. We were still young adults, finding our way in the world, and he had a conflict with my answer which was simply, "Happy."

He said, "No, like what do you want to DO?"

And my response was, "I don't know, but whatever it is I want to be happy."

He felt that "happy" was not a sufficient goal, nor could happiness be a goal and we discussed it at length. We eventually agreed to disagree and moved on.

Maybe 10 years later, he called and said, "I've been thinking about what you said and I agree."

He is an old friend, and our conversations NEVER end. They are "parliamentary," we merely "table" discussions. Without actually stating it, our conversations seem to be run by Robert's Rules of Order. Seriously. However, since no one actually takes notes and meetings are not scheduled, I was clearly at a loss as I stood with the telephone in my hand as my brain churned to recall what I had said and when. We had not spoken in a while. So when he clarified his statement, it was a combustible moment for me. My mind imploded with memories. I saw and felt the discussion of SO many years prior. WOW. I was humbled at the depth of our friendship and his commitment to exploration. He was still thinking about that. He remembered our disagreement. So many kids, years, and relationships later it was powerful enough for his mind to continue to consider this possibility. Wow. (Or maybe he was pretty darn bored. Hmm. I will stick with the former conclusion.)

Now, clearly, life has not always been in support of my personal commitment to happiness. But I remain steadfast. I have created many a mantra to remind myself of this commitment when happiness is but a mere memory. The last line of one favorite mantra is, "I am living my life, INjoy." I affirm this to myself on a daily basis. It has become my tagline. MANY of my friends have made it their own. I chuckle when I see it used by someone else. When I customize my personal checks, it is above the signature line. When I sign my personal emails, the closing is INjoy. One friend/author, David Rivera Jr., actually put it in one of his books, I think it was the fourth one. Imitation is the best form of flattery, dig it. So, I am now published. Sweet. LOL. I am cool with spreading this "virus."

People talk about wearing "rose colored" glasses. Well, joy is the lens through which I see my life and I consciously choose to live my life INjoy. Every day, every moment, every second. I commit to fully experiencing all things, painful or not, INjoy. As difficult as some life experiences are, I can learn from them. I seek out the joy and jump into it.

INjoy is an adverb, it modifies how I live. I hope you will join me as...

I am living my life
INjoy,

As difficult as some life experiences are, how can you choose to live life INjoy?

2

The more you open your heart to others, the more life becomes joyful.
— Debasish Mridha

There is something wonderful and scary about opening your heart. Especially as an adult. Your heart has been cut, bruised, and hopefully sewn back together. There are gaps in love for others and perhaps love for self. But on the flipside, when we embrace love we open ourselves to more. It is a thrilling roller coaster ride with all the ups and downs. I have fierce vivid memories of love and the stories I told myself. My love from high school, the betrayal, and the world ending. But the world did not end. The world as I knew it at that time ended. I learned. I built a new definition of my world and how love looked and showed up in my world.

Reflect on how love brings you joy today compared to the past.

3

If you are not speaking it, you are storing it, and that gets heavy. — Christina Isabel

I am often told that I am brave for telling my story. But my belief is that vulnerability is a superpower. If I'm committed to my health, I have to tell my story. The more I tell my story, the stronger I get. The stronger I get, the more I can support others. Supporting others brings me joy.

I learned this the hard way in junior high school. My sister and I are 11 years apart. So while my peers were doing teenager things and being teenagers and preteens, I was taking care of my younger sister. People said that she had to be my child, because a sister wouldn't care for a younger sister as lovingly as I did. And that story went somewhere and a young man who had a crush on me told everybody about how we had had sex and what a "freak" I was. I was still a virgin and being judged harshly for rumors. My boyfriend had his doubts as he was being judged as well. I learned it was really important to speak up and advocate for myself and not default to believing all that I hear.

What stories have you heard about yourself from others that stole your joy?

4

**It is not death that a man should fear,
but he should fear never beginning to live.
— Marcus Aurelius**

We all know that death is an inevitable part of life. But most of us are crippled when it happens in our lives. My daughter Siwe's death in 2011 put me on a path to live life differently. I wrote my own press release as a blog post shortly after she died, *Live the Life You Never Lived*. I shared it as my way of retreating so I could heal. I posted it on my blog, shared it widely, and then stopped answering my phone for a long while. The real call to action was from my daughter's weekly column, "Ask Siwe." The post below was published about six months before she died.

Q: *What can parents do or say that will keep their child(ren) inspired to pursue their dreams?*

A: Well, for one, it would help to know that your dreams came true. The problem is that we don't really have that. It is rare that you find a kid whose parent comes home from work with a smile and shares how grand their day was and how much they LOVE working there. We are surrounded by adults who are angry and unsatisfied with their work lives. No matter what you say to help us, it will sound empty because how are we supposed to make it with our dreams if you couldn't? We hate comparing ourselves to you, *ahem* "Older People," but this is one time when we can't help but compare.

I think what works best is just telling us how much you believe in us. Push us to do our best. Believe in us. Pardon me for sounding corny, but you gotta be there for us. No matter what.

Whew. Even if you are not a parent that will make you think about your life and how you appear to others, especially the youth in your life.

Take some time to reflect on your life as it is now compared to your dreams. Are you happy? What is ONE thing you can do today that would put you on the path to living the life of your dreams? Maybe it is something on your "bucket" list.

5

Give yourself permission to be where you are and grieve how you grieve. It's ok to not be ok. It is also ok to be happy. — #dionnesays

---

I am hard wired for joy. So, when something takes me down the rabbit hole to sadness it is a whole-body experience. There will be flickers of joy. I remember having good days in the midst of grief and someone said to me that I seemed like I was doing "too good." I countered that with, "I am good until I am not."

People will often judge you by their own personal experiences. But we receive their statements as truths and make ourselves wrong instead of assessing the source. Try this, acknowledge where the comment is coming from, and do your best not to take it personally. Quite often it has more to do with them than you. Perhaps they triggered a hidden belief you have about yourself. If someone told you that you were green, you'd probably shrug it off with ease because you know it is not true. If someone said you were a horrible person and not worthy of joy and you did not shrug that off in the same way, it is probably because some part of you believes that.

Take some time to solidify your opinions of yourself separate from outside forces. Write down a few of your best qualities as well as a few traits that you are less proud of. Focus on increasing the best qualities and diminishing the less endearing traits.

6

If you hit a wall, climb over it, crawl under it, or dance on top of it. — Unknown

I love this particular quote, because quite often I tell people the best choreography I have ever created is my life. I dance through situations, places, and ways of being quite masterfully. The fact that I started musical theater and dancing at five years of age has taught me how to move through spaces. Decades of dancing has given me the ability to move through the impossible with a smile on my face. Dancers move through the air and create ease, comfort, and often beauty.

What memory can you connect to? How can that experience help you move through a difficult situation with ease and grace?

7

But mommy, even Jill Scott says that we all cry when we feel pain. — Siwe Monsanto

Oh my goodness! Out of the mouth of babes. My daughter used to cry a lot. No, I really mean a lot! Forty-five minutes at a bare minimum. And when I would explain to her that it just wasn't normal and I needed her to use her words to explain to me what was going on so I could support her, it did nothing.

Back story. I am a die-hard avid Jill Scott fan. So, during our many road trips (with a limited selection of cassettes and CDs available), Jill Scott would be on repeat. As a result, my daughter, while still in the single digits, had gleaned enough to make this statement and use a Jill Scott song as the precedent to defend her right to cry.

Maybe Siwe was right. She was listening, learning, defending, and advocating for herself. We can all learn from the youth.

How can you better advocate for yourself in big ways
or small ways?

8

Every pair of eyes facing you has probably experienced something you could not endure. — Lucille Clifton

When I left the hospital after my daughter died, it was surreal. I was barely three blocks from my home and as I walked home, accompanied by my pastor, I kept looking around at the people. The sun was shining. People were moving around freely. Nothing had changed for them. I was so deeply connected to my trauma and my pain there was a major shift in how I saw other people. I knew that somebody else looking at me would just think, "There's a woman walking." As opposed to thinking, "There's a woman who is suffering deeply."

All of my insides were different. I felt my pain should be visible because my daughter had just died. I got really clear that each one of these other people had lived through some things that I couldn't see. They might have lived through some things that I couldn't imagine.

In that moment, I truly learned compassion. I am still more judgmental than I care to admit, but I self-manage my thoughts and actions with surprising speed.

How can you be more compassionate with others?

9

Be kind, for everyone you meet is fighting a hard battle. — Plato

Compassion has been an important part of my journey. As a young child, I consistently befriended the people who got picked on, the underdogs. The people who were made to feel oddly different and that they did not belong. I was considered short and fat. My mother was not the best at styling hair and my "parts" were not always straight. I did not like wearing sneakers or jeans. I did not fit in too well and the underdogs were my people. I was smart and liked talking to adults, so I was thought of as the "teacher's pet" and someone who clearly thought I was better than my peers. I had a weak bladder and always needed to go to the bathroom. These things were unforgivable sins in the 1970s. All of those experiences in elementary school helped me master sympathy.

These hurtful lessons stayed with me into adulthood. As an adult with all too many painful childhood memories,

I knew other people were dealing with some challenging times too.

How can you be more compassionate with yourself and others?

10

It is not selfish to be happy. It is your highest purpose. Your joy is the greatest contribution you can make to life on the planet. A heart at peace with its owner blesses everyone it touches. — Alan Cohen

---

South Bronx, New York. Junior high school. 1970s. I remember three boys always picking on me because I was so happy. They consistently tried to find ways to get me to stop smiling. It never worked. I laughed and smiled all the more, as I thought it was hilarious that my NOT smiling was so important to them. I wasn't into boys yet, so I just thought this was the weirdness of boys. Many years later, I learned that they actually liked me and wanted to get my attention. They all had crushes on me! Memories of those boys complaining and teasing me about being happy and smiling all the time made it clear to me that joy was important. How fascinating! I was a preteen in the South Bronx and my joy was so valuable it was worth stealing.

How valuable is your joy to you?

11

There are years that ask questions and years that answer. — Zora Neale Hurston

---

2009-2011 were the years in my life that asked a lot of questions.

There were 14 deaths in 11 months. Including my father, my grandfather, my ex-father-in-law, my ex-grandfather-in-law, my father-in-law, my mother-in-law, my mentor, and the list goes on.

Although I have never been in a boxing ring, during those years I could actually imagine what it's like to be physically punched and fall down. And every time you attempt to stand up, you are punched again and again. There was literally no time to mentally and emotionally catch my footing before I got the news that someone else died. I was working in financial services and Siwe was attempting suicide regularly.

She had been in and out of different pediatric psychiatric wards and emergency rooms with her suicide attempts, and I was still working. I was not yet divorced from my abusive ex-husband. I do not have the words to express how rough it was.

In 2011, Siwe, my daughter, died by suicide.

2012 was a year of answers. In retrospect, the 14 deaths in 11 months (February 2009-January 2010) were preparing me for my greatest loss, the death of my 15-year-old daughter. While accepting her death, I had an identity shift. I had to decide who I was in the world. How I would show up for myself and my sons. The world looked different and felt different. I was different. I left my 20-year career and became a full-time yoga teacher.

Reflect on your life. What years asked you questions? What years gave you answers? What did you learn?

12

I now see how owning our story and loving ourselves through that process is the bravest thing that we will ever do. — Brené Brown

The only story your life tells is yours. No matter how much our parents have tried to impress their hopes and their dreams for us into us, we live our lives to tell our personal stories.

From this quote, and other people telling me that it was brave, I have learned that I live my life as an open book. My mother did a great job imparting self-love and self-care to me. And people did a really great job on telling their story of their vision for me, so I wound up living my life loudly and authentically to dispel rumors — this became a habit that still serves me well today.

Even if you don't feel brave, find a way to tell your story today. Owning all aspects of yourself can create joy.

Make it a habit to share your story daily, even if the one person you tell today is yourself in the mirror.

13

**If you are going through hell, keep going.
— Winston Churchill**

I love this quote so much it's actually a magnet on the front door of my home. Even if I am physically being still, I am most often in a constant state of motion. I'm planning and creating a visual plan in my mind's eye to step into. That habit has served me well throughout the majority of my life, especially when there were challenges. This quote helped me learn that I didn't have to stop and overanalyze what was happening. This quote tells us not to get comfortable in misery. Do not stop and smell the flowers in hell. Keep moving in search of your joy. Movement, even slight, can take you closer to joy.

Even if your body feels crushed with the weight of life, how can you move towards joy? A phone call? A five-minute dance party? A stroll? Allow yourself movement.

14

Choose well. Your choice is brief and yet endless. — Goethe

I love tea. Whenever I have tea and I notice there's a quote, I'm so excited to read one of the quotes. My partner, Roger, is a jokester; he wouldn't let me read the quote on his tea bag. But he taped it to the mirror on "my side" in the bathroom. When I brushed my teeth that evening, he knew I'd look up and see it right at eye level. It stayed there for several years. I read it and my mind was just blown.

It was an immediate time warp of thoughts and memories about my choices. Choices with food, places with men and relationships, and choices with money. I could clearly think of so many choices that I felt were horrible. Choices that were not in my best interests that I feel have left me scarred forever.

I have had challenges with my weight off and on since childhood, I was considered short and fat. I kept thinking about all my choices that in my opinion, sucked. I was a big comfort food eater. And in my family, food is love. If something bad happens, you fix it by feeding the person. This quote helped me start thinking about how the choices I make today will impact me today, one, two, or five years from now.

What choice can you make today that will make you smile? What choice can you make that brings you closer to your goals?

15

You never know how strong you are until being strong is your only choice.
— Bob Marley

When I heard this quote years ago, I immediately reflected on all of Siwe's periods of hospitalization. I was a single mother of three children, a homeowner, and a landlady. I was active in an African dance company. I had a car in New York City without a place to park it. My cup and proverbial plate were running over, and things were a mess. I was in a constant state of forgetting something, failing on something, and not doing something on time. I was eating through my pain and gained 80 pounds on my 5'0" short self in two to three years.

But when I look back on it now, I was a badass! I know there's some part of us that is supposed to be humble and not really pat ourselves on the back or sing our own praises. But I really don't know how I did it.

I bet you have an experience in your life where you didn't know how you were going to move forward or how anything would get done, but one way or another it did get done.

Take a moment now to celebrate yourself for your strength, not your perceived weaknesses, but your actual strength. You have lived through some tough things. I applaud you, so applaud yourself and acknowledge that you're probably a badass too.

16

To sweat is to pray, to make an offering of your innermost self. Sweat is holy water, prayer beads, pearls of liquid that release your past. The more you dance... the more you sweat, the more you pray. The more you pray, the closer you are to ecstasy.
— Gabrielle Roth

I'm a dancer and a yoga teacher; my first yoga certification was in Bikram yoga (original hot yoga). Needless to say, I sweat a lot. I was taking a Bikram yoga class when the teacher read this quote and I was moved. As soon as I left the room, I immediately searched for it so I could have it in my repertoire. It spoke to something really deep in the depths of your body coming out. And maybe you don't always want it to come out, maybe it's not an opportune time.

I'm in menopause, so I will absolutely break out into a sweat while sitting still and it feels embarrassing — but it's my innermost self coming out. I find solace in

Gabrielle Roth defining sweat as "pearls of liquid that release your past." It was empowering to think that I could release my past when I sweat. It inspired me that my sweat was ok, and I can sweat more. This quote helped me make peace with my often untimely sweat.

What is that thing for you that you're often embarrassed by? How can you shift your perspective and tell a different story for it to be ok? If you are not embarrassed by anything about yourself, great! Is there something you can make peace with today?

17

**Writing is a way of continuing to hope...
perhaps for me, it is a way of remembering,
I am not alone. — Lucille Clifton**

One of the reasons I share so much personal information about myself is because every time someone says they've been through something similar, it affirms that I'm not alone. Whether I'm talking about a loved one dying by suicide, challenges with menopause, challenges with weight, challenges with parenting, feelings of inadequacy, et cetera, et cetera. Seeing that person in the audience nod and knowing they felt the same way too affirms that I'm not alone. So, I totally get this. I don't know if I find my writing as being hopeful and it almost feels like a data dump from my brain to give me a sense of freedom. Journaling, writing, putting things on social media, just getting it out of my head makes a big difference.

What can you do today to relieve some pressure from your brain? How can you affirm that you are not alone?

18

Painting is just another way of keeping a diary. — Pablo Picasso

Visual artists have a way of expressing themselves, their emotions, and what's going on in the world. Some people are able to read these pictures as some read a book. Perhaps that is why so many artists have pieces that are unfinished. We all have emotions that are incomplete, feelings and memories that we don't want to let go of that would paint a picture of who we are (or how we were) much too clearly. Even without a paintbrush we stop painting that picture, so we make a choice (consciously or unconsciously) to pause at a certain point in time. Being unfinished gives a better image than being a mess. It is better than being vulnerable with all of the emotions.

If I could paint pictures of my many diaries, some would be dark and stormy nights with thunder, fire, and brimstone! Others would be beautiful landscapes of water, flowers, and trees.

If you could paint a picture of your diary, of your deepest thoughts, what would it look like?

19

If you are silent about your pain, they will kill you and say you enjoyed it.
— Zora Neale Hurston

At some point I only saw myself as others saw me — and it was good, since everyone saw me as good. I was in a circle of people who saw me as amazing, special, talented, smart, and beautiful. So, I became intrigued with and married a man who wanted to possess all of my "magic" and told me it was "just beans." As he brainwashed me, I began to believe all the negative things he said. I was too fat. My breasts were too small and I should get silicone implants. I was unattractive, but smart. I did not keep the house clean enough, but I was good enough to raise his child. I needed to look a certain way when we left the house, but he would be proud to show me off to his co-workers and friends. I had to exercise three times a week. Those were rough years, abusive years. They were not physically abusive, but they were mentally and emotionally abusive. Now it is hard to believe that I thought he loved me. I was so touched when I got a birthday card from him and my gift was that he was not going to ask me to get my breasts augmented any more. But I stayed. I had made a decision long before we got married that I didn't want to be divorced. So, I stayed longer than I should have. A common story, I'm sure.

As I started to believe the ugliness he saw in me, it was killing me. I felt stifled, smothered, and I was literally dying on the inside with a smile on my face. But just before my spirit was crushed, I sat in our bathtub one night trying to figure out how I could get in bed with my husband. I realized that my wedding promise ("until death do us part") did not mean I had to let my spirit die. I made the decision to leave that night.

What pain are you silent about? How is that stifling your joy?

20

Thinking will not overcome fear but action will. — W. Clement Stone

I am an Aries and I can get really comfortable in my head, but the desire to complete goals gets me into action. I might not always make the best decisions, but I am constantly in action with my decisions. One of the elders in my community says, "Pray and move your feet."

Once I decided my marriage was over, I decided on how I would live.

Once I decided I was going to yoga teacher training, I started telling people to make myself accountable. (I had a letter of recommendation even before I had started my application!)

Analysis paralysis does not serve you. Even if it is calling someone for support or going for a walk, what action can you take that will move you out of fear?

21

**Do the thing you fear to do and keep on doing it... That is the quickest and surest way ever yet discovered to conquer fear.
— Dale Carnegie**

I became a yoga teacher because I fell in love with the practice that helped me heal physically from pneumonia and then emotionally from my daughter's death. Yoga was not something black people did. Suicide was not something black people did either. Such fallacies! I did not have a person in my community who had walked a path that felt right for me. I had a good job in a global financial services firm that so many people wanted. I had a house and three children. But to really live, I had to leave my job and follow my heart.

For nine weeks, I immersed myself in yoga teacher training while my boyfriend lived with and cared for my kids. It was insane and I loved it. I felt alive. I was happy.

What do you need support with to get over a fear? Who can help you with that? Do you know what your fears are? Do you have a desire to overcome them? Think of one small step you could take today towards conquering that fear.

22

We don't stop playing because we grow old. We grow old because we stop playing.
— George Bernard Shaw

I love playing. I loved being a child. I remember making a decision when I was young that I would be responsible, but I wouldn't be a "grup." (*Star Trek* reference from Season 1, Episode 8.) It was important to me to have this level of playfulness and to have fun. I was an only child until I was 11 and the grown-ups always seemed so upset about something. The blessing of being the only child was I could be in the room with all the adults and hear everything. I learned to be visible yet invisible. I learned to listen and hold secrets so I could keep listening. It was then that I decided I wouldn't be the kind of "grup" that people couldn't tell secrets to. I decided that it was good to listen and hold the secrets because I could stay in the room with the people, play, and have fun. Some of that still holds true today.

At one point my kids told me that I wasn't fun, and I was thankful for the honesty. I remembered the seriousness of the "grup" and my promise to myself. I had to change. I knew I had succeeded when my youngest son told me I should "grow up" and another time asked me why couldn't I dress like other moms?

What decisions did you make as a child? Do they serve you now? Are you willing to change them if they don't?

23

**The most sophisticated people I know —
inside they are all children. — Jim Henson**

I think I gained the most popularity as I said to my students, "Let's *play* yoga." Such a minute change in language. But as I said to them, it's so much more fun to play yoga. If you think that we are doing yoga, there is an implied need to conquer, to master, or to persevere. But we're less attached to the outcome if we're just playing. Children play and still learn.

When did you stop playing? And why? How can you invite play back into your life?

24

**It always seems impossible until it is done.
— Nelson Mandela**

I graduated from high school when I was 16 years old. I wasn't really a good student. I was a C student who graduated early. But there was something special about being young and going to college, especially in the neighborhood that I grew up in. A young black girl raised by her grandmother and her mother, who never met her biological father, graduated from high school at 16 and went to college. From the South Bronx. Fort Apache. Millbrook Projects.

I did not graduate from Old Dominion University (ODU). I left early that first year for family reasons. I was a drop-out. But I ultimately graduated magna cum laude with a Bachelor of Science in Accounting from Hunter College – CUNY (City University of New York). That four-year degree happened in three parts at two universities. And I was a married pregnant mother of one working at Morgan Stanley when it happened, but it happened. I started ODU in 1983 and graduated from Hunter College in 1996, shortly before my second child was born.

I did it. So, I can't say it was impossible — but I was definitely told when I dropped out of college that I would never go back. I, however, did not attach myself the impossibility of it.

What did you want to do that you were told was not possible? How can you shift your perspective?

25

All life is interrelated. We are all caught in an inescapable network of mutuality, tied into a single garment of destiny. Whatever affects one directly, affects all indirectly.
— Dr. Martin Luther King Jr.

Therein lies the rub. In certain countries, we've been taught that we are individuals. That we should take care of ourselves and we get so caught up in the ME of things, we don't see the WE. If I'm suffering and we are in a community together on this planet, suffering will impact you in some way. Sight unseen and voice unheard, there's a collective energy that we create.

The 1946 holiday film, *It's a Wonderful Life*, drives that message home beautifully as the lead character sees what life looks like without him.

Know that you're not alone. Your thoughts and your life make a difference because we are all connected.

How can you expand yourself to see and feel how connected you are to all that is? Let that thought seep into your body. Write about how that feels.

26

If you carry joy in your heart, you can heal any moment. — Carlos Santana

Learning to transmute pain into joy has helped me heal any moment. And as I wrote this book, there were so many stories of grief, death, abuse, and loss that I questioned whether the title should be about joy. And this quote is what made it clear for me that it should, because the joy in my heart is what has allowed me to heal after so much loss in my life. I have lived through so many challenges and choose joy. I could list each trauma here in detail or I could focus on the abundance created.

From each trauma, I gained strength and perseverance. I asked to learn the lessons so I would not have to repeat them. I remember calling my abusive ex-husband to thank him when I got my lesson from that marriage.

That was an interesting conversation, but I felt it was important for me to express gratitude and be in communication with him since we were co-parenting. I learned from that interaction that is sometimes better to thank people in silence.

Find the silver lining in your pain. Who or what can you thank for your lessons?

27

Find joy in everything you choose to do. Every job, relationship, home... It's your responsibility to love it, or change it.
— Chuck Palahniuk

If you haven't done so already, now might be a great time to write some stuff down. Make a list of the things that do not bring you joy that you have been doing on a regular basis. The challenge is that your identity might be keeping you from your joy. What are you doing the most? Joy can be found in the actions you are repeating. So set a timer, give yourself five minutes to write things down that do not bring your joy, and look at how often you've been doing things that frustrate you or do not bring you joy.

When I realized I had permission to disconnect from places, people, and things that did not bring me joy, it gave me the freedom to create a life filled with things that do bring me joy.

Look at how you spend your time. What things do you do, on a regular basis, that do not bring you joy? How can you make shifts to have more time and space to experience joy?

28

If you're not having a good time, find something else that gives you some joy in life. — Penny Marshall

I spent 20 years in financial services between two different companies because I had to pay my bills. I was raised that you graduated from high school, then college, and got a "good job." I took the slow road on that journey, but I did it. Check. Check. Check. I even bought a house and became a landlord. Check. Check.

But I was not happy. Where was happiness on the list to check off? It was not on the list I was taught... So, I added it. I had my 9-5 job. And then I created a life of things done after work that brought me joy.

I started doing things in the evening and on the weekends that made me happy: friends, family, dance classes, reading, writing, coaching, cooking, learning, self-help, self-growth, and self-improvement. So, now I had a bunch of things that gave me joy — but I was too exhausted all the time.

I am so thankful for my therapist and how she masterfully helped me see the toxicities in my life. It took quite some time and a few tragedies for me to leap, but she was the first person to give me permission to let go of things that brought me down instead of lifting me up. She was instrumental in ensuring that I leave my career in financial services, as it was impacting my health negatively.

Make a list of things. Things you do (or have done) that don't bring you joy. If you are still doing those things, take some time to reflect. Ask yourself a few questions. Why am I still doing this? What can I do instead of this? Who can I talk to about this? Who is in my corner? How can they help me make a change?

29

There are those who give with joy, and that joy is their reward. — Khalil Gibran

At some point, I remember thinking I was doing too much. I had spread myself too thin. Then I realized that I am a serial helper. It helps me to help others and if I'm not helping others, I do not feel as fulfilled. Find those people and surround yourself with them. Perhaps if people are not your thing, surround yourself with things that will bring you joy. Tell yourself you deserve joy, because you do. Joy is your birthright. Say it repeatedly until you believe it.

Do you have people in your life who give joy? How do you feel when you're around them? Are you the person in everyone else's life who gives joy? Do you feel rewarded? Ask these questions and more. Listen in the stillness of your mind and your body. Hear and feel your answers. Keep making lists and listening to the silence.

30

Sometimes your joy is the source of your smile, but sometimes your smile can be the source of your joy. — Thich Nhat Hanh

I always heard from my mother and my godfather that I had a million-dollar smile, that I had a smile that would light up any room. Certainly, one would think these are things that family members would say to a young child. Oddly enough as I got older and continued to hear these things, I started to believe them. Then when I met someone who smiled at me and my heart lit up. Then I saw how others lit up when my daughter smiled. I finally got it. Sometimes you are so blessed to bear witness to a smile so bright, that it ignites joy in others. Sometimes it is your smile that will create joy for you or for others.

Even if you're not sure of this truth, please share your smile as a gift of joy to the world. Let it radiate from deep within you. Your eyes can smile too.

When was the last time a smile bubbled up from inside of you and you could not contain it? Make a list of things that make you smile from the inside out.

31

To get the full value of joy, you must have someone to divide it with. — Mark Twain

---

Please note, I've spent the better majority of my life being a single extrovert. I have failed at many intimate relationships, but I am a people person. I do draw energy and get charged from being with and around people. So, with this quote, I am not stating that it needs to be a romantic partnership.

You are one of a kind. You have a unique gift that only you can share with the world. Your joy is magnified when shared on your terms.

Share your joy with a loved one (family, friend or intimate partner). Share your joy with a cashier, a customer service representative, a stranger. Spread joy and watch it multiply.

The joy you share will come back to you. How can you spread joy today?

32

Comparison is the death of joy.
— Mark Twain

Every time I've compared myself to someone else, I come up feeling inadequate. Sometimes I think about it so much it becomes a self-fulfilling prophecy; I become sad. And because I'm sad, I become unproductive. And because I'm unproductive, when I see other people and the beautiful things that they're doing in the world, I feel inadequate. Sometimes, it's not even good for me to compare myself to myself!

Honor this moment in this space where you are. Right here, right now, you are breathing. You're reading this because in some way you were connected to the idea of creating joy in your life. Pat yourself on the back. Tell yourself you are worthy of joy. Create joy without comparison.

What or who do you compare yourself to? How does that feel?

33

There are souls in this world who have the gift of finding joy everywhere, and leaving it behind them when they go.
— Frederick William Faber

Joy is quantifiable. And if you're that sort of person, your income will increase. You will have longevity in your career. In the same way that higher education benefits your career, being nice benefits your life.

It was only when I was resigning from my position as a vice president at a large financial services firm, did I start to realize what an asset I was to my department. It was not my mathematical acumen or knowledge of the field. I brought peace and joy wherever I went. It was not on my resume, nor could I explain it in an interview. But that was the reason I was passed over each time there was a workforce reduction (layoffs). My job could have been eliminated, but the essence that was uniquely me is what I was really paid for.

I was the person who spread joy when I was in a room. Above and beyond the project we were working on and my technical skill set, my essence was necessary. It was felt and seen when I was there and missed when I was not. I asked about their family, their days, their house, their kids, and their pets. I added an integral level of human connection to every project. In a restaurant, I make sure I know the waiter's name. I read the cab driver's name. Even as I teach, I ask my students about their loved ones. Kayla about her dog Scout. Mana about her daughter Rasa. Holly about her cats Chewy and Mosby. Amy about her cats Jack and Benny. Building human connection is a great way to move beyond the mundane tasks you're working on. Spreading joy raises the vibration in the room.

How do you raise the vibration in a room?

34

Joy lies in the fight, in the attempt, in the suffering involved, not in the victory itself. — Mahatma Gandhi

In different countries, this might present differently. However, if you were born and raised in the United States, it sometimes feels as though the victory was what was most valued. As I thought about the book I wanted to write and the stories I wanted to tell, it was all about the journey. All too often people see and perceive me as "always being happy" and I have it "all together." But the truth is, joy is something I choose to fight for on a daily basis. Any success I have amassed came at a cost, and with substantial work. There are still many days I am dealing with a myriad of personal conflicts regarding ways to create and maintain joy when external (or internal) factors attempt to diminish my expansive joy. I acknowledge that sometimes the person that's getting in my way is me. Joy lies in the journey.

Are you getting in your way? Is joy something you are willing to work towards? How can you create a clear path to joy?

35

Joy is not in things; it is in us.
— Richard Wagner

I got this while I was living in a one-bedroom New York City apartment. I was married with two children and living in an apartment that could probably fit in what is currently my kitchen and dining room. Two adults and two children living in a small space crammed with toys and books, creating a life, and my husband was miserable. And in his misery, I got the deepest and greatest lesson that it really didn't matter what we had or where we were: I could be happy with him.

Happiness is so elusive if it's attached to a thing. We see it in the distance like a lightning bug we cannot catch. I'll be so happy if I get this promotion. I'll be happy when I buy this house. I'll be happy once I get married. I'll be happy after I have my first child. The lightning bug (joy) keeps moving.

Attach your joy to your existence. Be happy you are alive. And with each breath of life, there is hope for more joy and more life.

List the things or people you are grateful for. Add to this list, read it and repeat it aloud often.

36

You can cry and close your mind, be empty and turn your back. Or you can do what [they] would want: smile, open your eyes, love and go on. — David Harkins

People die. This quote is a gender-neutral excerpt from a longer poem about ways we can respond to the death of a loved one.

There's been a great deal of loss in all of our lives, whether it's an emotional loss, a physical loss as in someone's death, or a relationship ending. There's so much grief and when it's specifically death, I reflect on what that person's contributions were and what will mine be? What is it that I can do to live as they did? Or how can I create a legacy that they would appreciate?

What are some positive traits or contributions from people you have lost? Which one of those things could you continue for them and also for you?

37

Death is a reminder for the living to live.
— #dionnesays

So many things and people have died. It's important for us today to have clarity on what's important in our lives. My losses have given me tremendous clarity on how to move forward powerfully to manifest and create the joy I seek in my life. Below is my blog post from the losses in the global pandemic.

I have been blogging about death for many years, but it seems truly relevant on a global level now. In general, death seems to be the most misunderstood part of life. The gamut of emotions felt after someone's death are tremendous. (Google the 5 stages of grief.) While there are so many ways of processing death culturally, life in the time of "the Rona" has turned everything around. People are not able to process death and gather in the ways they would otherwise.

The grief we are processing is not only the deaths of various people we have lost, but we are also grieving our lives as we knew them. Loss of jobs, loss of income, living in fear of touch, et cetera, et cetera, ad infinitum. While texting with a dear friend, she pointed out to me how she finds comfort in my words. She implored me to share them.

Here are my truths around death that comfort me. I have written some version of this in more sympathy cards and Facebook pages than I can recall over the years.

I believe that when someone dies, their essence is in the very air we breathe. TAKE DEEP BREATHS. They are with you in a different way. The love you felt for them (and them for you) still exists. Close your eyes, breathe deeply, and revel in the memories you have shared.

#loveNEVERdies

If there is something you did not say or do with them...SAY IT NOW. DO IT NOW.

All of the deaths in my personal life have taught me, have shaped me. #siwelives

I have become the Queen of Acceptance. I live these words daily; they are not merely hashtags. I do live my life urgently NOW. I am clear that tomorrow is

NOT promised. Grief is a personal process and I am good when I am good, and I am not when I am not. It is ok to NOT be ok. I give myself permission to be where I am. It seems simple, but it is not always. I have my "grief toolkit" and I use resources readily available online from the American Foundation for Suicide Prevention.

Even if things have changed and you are mourning, you are here. You are reading this. You have breath. You have life. What will you do with this gift? I am not pushing productivity. I am promoting self-care, self-awareness, self-acceptance. I can be a resource for you. You are not alone. Let's talk.

I am living my life
INjoy,

Chief Joy Connector

#loveneverdies
#livelifeurgentlynow
#tomorrowisnotpromised
#griefisapersonalprocess
#deathisareminderforthelivingtolive

Has someone you love died? How can you live your life in a way that honors them and creates joy in your life?

38

I define joy as a sustained sense of well-being and internal peace — a connection to what matters. — Oprah Winfrey

Figuring out what really matters to you is a big part of this journey called life. So, take some time to define that and it will change — even if you write down today a list of 100 things that are important to you, people who are important to you, and ways of being that are important to you. The list might change, but it gives you a foundation to build from. When you know what matters to you, you can then create your joy, magnify your joy, and let it come from the inside out into the world.

Are you an extrovert, introvert, or ambivert? Do you need time to charge with people, alone, or both? Ask yourself questions, and listen for the answers.

Make a list of at least 20 things, people, and ways of being that are important to you.

39

A flower blossoms for its own joy.
— Oscar Wilde

When I see myself as a flower, it's easier to smile. And sometimes my smile comes from a deep place within. Sometimes, my smile comes from external stimulation. Seeing something beautiful. Smelling something fragrant. Tasting something delicious. Hearing a sound: laughter, birds chirping, music, or a song. Feeling something that brings comfort. That's the sort of smile that's just for me, a secret that grows from a place only I know the story to.

How can you be a flower and bloom for your joy? What is the water that helps you grow?

40

He who has family and friends is richer than he who has money. — African proverb

Sometimes, there are quotes that make me question if they were created from a place of lack. And other times, I feel a deep sense of power in that. I have friends, I have family, and I do feel as though I'm rich. Plus, it also brings me great joy to work to create financial prosperity as well to partner with the wealth that I already have.

Certain cultures speak to prosperity in connection to physical tangible things with price tags on them. There's a lifeless, spiritless identity attached to wealth that seems devoid of family and friends or, rather, devoid of family and friends who are sincerely there without their own interests in mind.

How can you create a circle of people who know your soul and reflect you? A tribe that will support your values, feel enriched by your presence, and perhaps even challenge you to grow?

41

Grief is a personal process. — #dionnesays

While grieving, there are days that you'll be at peace and smile. There are days where even if you were to paint a smile on your face, the weight of your sadness would melt it off. There are days where you'll do nothing but move from one side of the bed to the other, and then there are days where you're so highly functional and supportive of others that you will be judged that you're doing too well. There might be days that turn into weeks with crying that just won't stop, and you'll be judged that you're taking too long to heal. I was judged so much. I trusted the process and gave myself permission to be where I was. I did not know how I would get there, but I knew there was another side of the process.

If I was happy, so be it. If I was sad, so be it. If I needed to excuse myself and go to the bathroom and cry for 30 minutes, so be it. I did not always respond when I was judged. But if I did, it was with these words: *Grief is a personal process.* I still offer this truth freely to those who have lost loved ones.

What is your grieving process? How has it evolved over the years? Where did it come from?

42

The dance is not where we lose ourselves. But where we find ourselves.
— Gabrielle Roth

One of the first signs of life when we are born into the world is movement and sound. We cry and move, which signals to the people around us that this new life that has come into the world is ok. Whether you think you can dance or not, you do dance. You dance through life at your rhythm to your beat.

When you've lost your way, play a song and have a private dance party to find yourself. Keep moving with the music until something awakens inside of you and you find yourself.

Have a dance party today just because. Create a list of songs that move your body and mind.

43

A good head and a good heart are always a formidable combination.
— Nelson Mandela

A good head and a good heart can sometimes feel like a curse. There's so much compassion and having a good heart, you might not always do what seems logical. The shortest way to a destination might not always be the most compassionate. But the ties you'll create and the bonds with other humans and with the planet will make you a force to reckon with.

What can you do today to support your heart? What can you do today to strengthen your head?

44

There comes a point where we need to stop just pulling people out of the river. We need to go upstream and find out why they're falling in. — Desmond Tutu

Revolutionaries have a different way of seeing the world and thinking. I'm not just talking about war as revolution, but innovation as revolution. Innovation decides that there's a different way, a better way to do something. We all have challenges in our life and we only know how to do things the way we know how to do them.

Although I am short, I have always been "big boned." My family line was short and thick, period. We cooked, ate, and lived a certain way. We had similar health issues (high blood pressure, diabetes, obesity, et cetera). I thought I would always struggle with weight since we all did. This was all I knew. It took years for me to *right-size my body* and then *right-size my life*.

Are there challenges in your life that seem familial, age-old, or you've accepted it as, "This is just who I am or how I am?" Write these things down, take some time to "go upstream and find out why." Observe how other groups of people or families do a particular thing. Decide what you are willing to try and be open to a different possibility, a different outcome.

45

If you want to give birth to your true self, you are going to have to dig deep down into that body of yours and let your soul howl. Sometimes you have to take a leap of faith and trust that if you turn off your head, your feet will take you where you need to go. — Gabrielle Roth

There are so many schools of thought about how different parts of your body have a brain. This makes me think of my feet as having a brain that is connected to my spirit. Intuition. There are moments where you will struggle, and you will get stuck. And if you are able to physically move, go for a walk. If you are not able to go outside for a walk, move in your house; shake your arms and legs. If your body will not move, close your eyes, go deep within, and move throughout the planet with ease in your mind. For most people, feeling trapped brings inexplicable pain.

Find ways to feed your imagination. When you feel stuck, go somewhere. Even if you cannot physically move, roam freely into the infinite vastness of your mind.

Let your imagination run wild. Trust your intuition and let your feet (or your mind) take you somewhere unexpected. Write about what you learned, felt, or saw.

46

Energy moves in waves. Waves move in patterns. Patterns move in rhythms. A human being is just that, energy, waves, patterns, rhythms. Nothing more. Nothing less. A dance. — Gabrielle Roth

In this second half of my life, I have found my rhythm. I didn't know I had found it until the whole world shut down with COVID-19 and I got to see how my patterns and rhythms supported my joy. Take some time to try new things, get lost, and find your way. Be vulnerable and share your likes and dislikes with people who can reflect them back to you when you have forgotten. They'll help you come back to your rhythm, your dance, your song. And if perhaps you don't want to leave it with a person, write it down in a journal. When you go back and read your writings, you'll find yourself there.

Collect patterns from a time in your life when you were happy. Create rhythms from those patterns and use them in your life now.

47

Every strike brings me closer to a home run. — Babe Ruth

I'm not sure how you define failure, but I'm confident that I have failed and embarrassed myself in more ways than I care to share. I was a bed wetter for far longer than I care to share. I love people and I loved having sleepovers. So, can you imagine wanting to be with your best friend at her house and not wanting to go to sleep because you know your bladder will betray you? I lied and lied, and would find ways to make up some falsehood about what happened, like I spilled a drink in the bed. Perhaps they knew. Perhaps my mother had already told them. But I was proud and I was embarrassed and ashamed of being a bedwetter so I lied.

Those strikes made me resilient in finding alternate ways to be with people I loved until I was willing to share the truth.

I love dancing. I have been in several dance companies.

But I do not remember choreography well. I strike out in that area to this day. I work extremely hard on the choreography until it I get it. I do not give up on myself. The strikes in rehearsal or dance classes have make me physically stronger with great cardio as I repeat the steps over and over again.

What have you learned from your strikes? How have your skills been honed?

48

Reality is created by the mind. We can change our reality by changing our mind. — Plato

I love the concept that I can create my reality with my thoughts. Everything begins with the decision. I can decide to be successful or I can decide to be a failure. And I also define what success is and what failure is, and I can shift that. If I look at my current reality and decide it is phenomenal, I'll get more of what I have by creating that energy of gratitude in the universe. And if I decide everything is horrible, then no matter what comes my way I will see as horrible. Like this fabulous scene I recall in the movie *What Dreams May Come* from back in the 80s when there were VHS cassettes. Robin Williams and his wife were both dead, and he was trying to bring her out of hell so they could be together. But no matter what he said to her, her reality was that of the glass being half empty.

Is your glass half empty? Is your glass half full? Neither

answer is wrong, but does what you choose support the reality you desire?

Write a few things down that you can change your mind about that will give you a more peaceful joy-filled reality.

49

Life is change. Growth is optional. Choose wisely. — Author Unknown

Perhaps each one of us comes to the planet with a certain number of things that are predetermined. Like the age old conversation of nature versus nurture. With what we are given, we have choices. Things are going to continue to change around us. People, places, weather, economies, friends, and family are constantly swirling and moving. If we are not able to make adjustments as everything changes around us, it could feel like a tornado. We could feel lost and defeated, but there's something special about choosing to grow; you can lean into the changes and find new ways of being.

On a daily basis, are you choosing growth? Without judgment, become aware of what your choices are. How do you respond to changes in your life? Do you choose to grow, lean into the changes and find new ways of being or do you get lost and feel defeated?

50

When you finally realize that nothing is permanent in this life you will become more tolerant, more forgiving and less judgmental. — Mufti Menk

I think this goes both ways. Sometimes people can be too tolerant almost to the point of being like a doormat, and that doesn't work for bringing you closer to joy. I do agree there is a certain sense of peace to accepting things as they are. The forgiveness and acceptance parts are more like accepting things and people as they are. Like you won't get mad at the Sun for being hot, because that's what it does. So, if somebody is a selfish narcissist, you're not going to be upset with them for being who they are. You may make different choices about how often you are in their presence and what you allow them to do with and for you. So, I think the forgiveness and the tolerance come from the acceptance of things and people being what they're supposed to be. Babies cry, they poop in diapers, and you don't get mad at that.

What are some things in your life that consistently frustrate you? What can you accept about them? What can you change?

A SPECIAL BONUS FROM dionne:
101 Ways to Live Life INjoy Journal

You are halfway through **101 Ways to Live Life INjoy**! Hopefully you've had some moments of reflection and found a few quotes that resonate with you. You are on your way to connecting to both yourself and others in a spirit of growth, health, and compassion.

In the spirit of giving, I created this special bonus to add to your joy toolkit... ***The 101 Ways to Live Life INjoy Journal*** will help you capture your aha moments and reflections from the book so you can implement them faster and more easily. **#LiveLifeINjoy**

Just go to the link below and tell us where to send it.
JoyousOcean.com/journal

I'm rooting for you! I look forward to hearing about your breakdowns as well as your breakthroughs!

Here's to living life
INjoy,

Dionne C. Monsanto
Chief Joy Connector
dionne@joyousocean.com

51

Close your eyes, fall in love.
Stay there. — Rumi

It was important to me as a mental health advocate to bring up some things that are on the edge of truth for me. Closing your eyes if you're dealing with PTSD (post-traumatic stress disorder) can be scary. You may see things that you're not in the space to fall in love with.

My father was in the Vietnam War. He never talked about what he experienced or what he lived through. But from watching movies and television shows as well as watching him as an insomniac and a functional alcoholic until he died, I know there were some things he didn't want to see and he couldn't fall in love with. There are times when I can close my eyes and listen to music and create imagery to fall in love with, but there is a certain level of intentionality that has to go along with closing your eyes.

If you're uncomfortable with closing your eyes or even believing that you can fall in love with what shows up in your mind's eye, try an open-eyed meditation. Simply walking in silence. Sitting still and staring at a candle flame for one minute. As you're cooking, staring at the flame on the stove for two minutes. Don't make yourself wrong if you're not able to close your eyes and fall in love with what you see right now. It's ok.

What do you see when you close your eyes? Write about that.

52

Nothing can harm you as much as your own thoughts unguarded. — Buddha

This is exactly the issue with many mental health diagnoses. At least 25% of the human population is dealing with a mental health challenge that may or may not be diagnosed and they may or may not be able to guard their thoughts. I don't have a mental health diagnosis that I'm aware of, but depression and anxiety do run deep in my family. During the pandemic that began in 2020, I started to see various habits and rituals and ways of being that I had in place and watched them unravel. And as the pandemic moved into 2021, I became keenly aware of the fragility of my mental health and how much I had created self-care rituals and a circle of friends to support me being strong. My mind is guarded. I can see my unraveling when it begins and reach into my self-care toolkit to take the first step towards repair.

It took me years to build my self-care tool kit. I started in the late 1990s! And when I became a certified life coach in 2009 and my daughter died in 2011, I got to see how strong the kit and the community I had built was. If you want more information about self-care toolkits and how to build them, send me a message. I love hearing from my readers, students, and clients.

Do you have a self-care toolkit? If yes, what is in your self-care toolkit? Or who is in your self-care toolkit? If not, start with one thing that you know lifts your spirits and build from there.

53

There is only one thing that makes a dream impossible to achieve: the fear of failure.
— Paulo Coelho

You might not believe this, but I've never had that fear of failure. I feel like I should ask my mom about this, but her memory is failing her these days. When I think of myself as a child, I would try something and get it wrong and laugh at myself. If I redefine failure as fear of disappointing myself, then there's a lot of stuff I didn't or don't do. There's a level of perfectionism or "should" that has existed in my life, but not nearly as much now (especially after Siwe's death). If I haven't mentioned it before, there are different time factors in my life. Before my daughter's death (BSD), after my daughter's death (ASD), before COVID-19 (BC), and after COVID-19 (AC).

I am generally too slow to start. My dreams have died in the waiting room. That place where my brain is waiting for things to be just right — the perfect time, the perfect place. I honestly don't know where I got that belief from, but I see it in others as well. I have come to learn, in AC life, that the time is now. All of the deaths helped me learn that tomorrow is not promised. And as my junior high school teacher would say, live life urgently now.

What would you do if you weren't afraid of failing? (I did one of mine! You're reading this book.) What is one step that you can take towards doing it?

54

Be yourself. Everyone else is already taken.
— Oscar Wilde

I have struggled to fit in most of my life. As the oldest child of the youngest girl, I was surrounded by people much older than me. My parents were my grandmother and my mother. I was a child of the "Children should be seen and not heard" era. I learned to master that concept very young. I got to hear about who was sleeping with whom. (Please imagine me, a seven-year-old girl sitting on the floor pretending to be deeply immersed in reading a book — but really trying to understand why sleeping with some-body was bad. I slept with my cousins all the time, and I slept with my mom and sometimes my grandmother.) Listening helped me a great deal with my vocabulary. I had to figure out how to spell words like affair, wedlock, and bastard, so I could look them up. This is probably why I have a good memory to date. When around my cousins, aunties, uncles, and friends of the family I learned to listen, learn, and hold secrets. I learned that you were valued and trusted when you could hold a secret.

Can you see that little girl? Now, take that same child and put her around children her age. Can you see her clearly? I just did not fit in. I didn't play the same games or read the same books. I read about astrology, Greek mythology, and Aesop's Fables. I stayed up late and I watched scary movies: *Chiller Thriller*, Vincent Price, and Alfred Hitchcock. I read Edgar Allan Poe. To my peers, I was weird. I don't think I found my tribe, my people until I got into theater and dance. They were weird like me. And then I got to see that so many people who were famous in the world didn't fit in anywhere either. This quote (even though there's lots of conversation about if it really was Oscar Wilde) makes me really happy and to tell the truth, I think that's the case for so many people. Being yourself might be really difficult in your current circle of people, but that's forcing you to find the right circle of people, places, and things.

How are you not being yourself? How can you experience freedom and own all of you?

55

The cure for anything is salt water: sweat, tears, or the sea. —Isak Dinesen

A dear friend of mine who spoke at my daughter's funeral gave me this quote. I was doing a challenge. I created it for myself and decided that I was going to do 365 yoga classes in 365 days. I did it. It was extremely challenging, but I did it. And she sent me this quote and it was like, "Wow!" I sweated so much that year and it was definitely my body shedding the tears that my eyes didn't cry. I think one of the reasons I'm so obsessed with movement, dance, and yoga is that it's all physical activity. Aerobic activity is moving at a pace in which sadness, depression, and anxiety can't catch up with me. Sometimes, my business protects me from the areas of my brain better left in the dark.

Tears. I don't like to cry, to shed them from my eyes. I'm not sure who does. I've never been good at crying, if there's such a thing. As a performer I've had roles where tears were required and it took a lot to get them to come out, so that's what I mean by it's not easy for me.

Sweat. Well, sweat comes easy for me. And when I was growing up, sweat was considered so unladylike. But I loved running; I loved physical activities. So, I did tend to sweat a lot. And then I became a Bikram yoga teacher. Clearly, exercising for 90 minutes in a room that's heated to 105°F with 40% humidity causes me to sweat a lot! I fit in!

Sea. The ocean. I have loved the ocean all of my life. As I recall, my first time being in an airplane flying above the ocean was to go to visit my family in St. Thomas, the United States Virgin Islands. And the clouds were magical. But getting to walk on the beach and be barefoot in the sand and in the ocean was a level of bliss beyond comparison.

What cures you the most? Sweat? Tears? The ocean? Why? Spend some time reflecting on that today. Create time to do the one that heals you the most. Sweat, cry, or connect with the sight, sound, or smell of the ocean.

56

I am not the same having seen the moon shine from the other side of the world.
— Author Unknown

Travel is educational. Travel is transformational. Travel is inspirational.

I absolutely love experiencing nature, people, and things. Food in a different destination. And just as much as I love experiencing all those things, I despise packing. Like packing is generally anxiety producing, because I like my things and I don't know what to leave. Managing time zones is fascinating as well. I have spent long periods of time in other countries and therefore time zones. Speaking to someone before you go to bed but it is day time for me is still mindboggling.

If we always stay in one place, we seem to think that our perspective is *the* perspective. Sometimes looking at the same situation from a different location can give you a different perspective. It is the same moon whether you are in Australia, Africa, or Antarctica; it will be the same situation that you're facing, but from a different view.

Traveling might not be getting in a car, a bus, or an airplane. It might be going for a walk and looking at the situation from a different angle from a different place.

Where have you traveled to? How did it change you? Where do you want to travel to? When will you go? If you are not physically able to travel, how can you shift your perspective?

57

How can anyone be against love?
— Malcolm X

There is such an innocence in that question. Let me make the disclaimer that I did not look up the context in which he said that. So, when I think about someone being against love I can actually think of a lot of reasons. Some of them might be selfish; some of them might be protective. When I think of what's commonly called puppy love or young love, I think of my daughter who had been so badly bruised; she had been the victim of sexual violence twice before she was 12 years old. When she wanted to start dating, she was so mentally fragile I was absolutely against it. I would tell her that it didn't matter to me who she was dating, she was not emotionally stable enough to date and it wasn't a good idea. She was someone who loved fiercely with all her mind, body, spirit, soul, and things.

Another example is of me, before I married Siwe's father. I was dead set in my decision to marry him regardless of the friends and family who advised against it. They could see it wasn't a good fit and he was not a healthy choice for me. But the combination of being Aries stubborn, goal-oriented, and set in my ways in my twenties made me marry the wrong person, and I had to learn the hard way.

So, I definitely think a lot of people can be against love and they might sometimes have good reasons.

Have you ever been against love? Do you know someone who was against love? Why?

58

You are never strong enough that you don't need help. — Cesar Chavez

This quote has a double negative. Translation:

YOU ARE STRONG ENOUGH THAT YOU DO NEED HELP.

Do you know the song, *With a Little Help from My Friends?* Sing it with me, "I get by with a little help from my friends." I have changed that to #igetbywithaLOTofhelpfromyfriends. Are you comfortable asking for help? If you are, how did you get to that point? If you are not comfortable asking for help, when did that happen and why did that happen?

I am generally supporting and helping others. My earliest memory of helping was asking to do the dishes at five years old and caring for my younger cousins at nine years old. In almost every situation, I step up and lean in to assist. However, I am still not good at asking for help. I have gotten better, but it is not second nature. This is a loud reminder for both of us.

You are strong enough that you do need help.

I hired an organizer to help with my house. Ten five-hour sessions over several months locked in better habits. I hired two different people to help me to write and publish this book. I recruited my friends to zhuzh up my NYC backyard into our "country home" escape. We created an oasis to get through the lockdown in NYC by safely distancing outdoors.

What could you accomplish if you asked for or hired help? Make a list and start asking or hiring.

59

In every seed of good there is always a piece of bad. — Marian Wright Edelman

I love water. Drinking water, immersing my body in water, swimming in the ocean, etc. My favorites are mineral water and salt water. Heavy waters. Water can heal you and water can drown you. You can float on water and you can die in water.

Love can go so far and so deep that people become obsessive and sometimes dangerous. Some may counter that it is obsession and therefore not love. But in the mind of that person, it is love.

Dr. Joy DuGruy speaks extensively on post-traumatic slave syndrome. There are a number of ways of being and parenting that so many oppressed populations take on that are not healthy for children. But these parents have learned such behaviors out of protection and love. You wanted that child to be safe, so you made them scared of going out or going past a certain place. Those parents instilled fear in their child and diminished the child's talents, so they wouldn't be sold. They had to parent in such a way that everything and everyone they loved seemed worthless, so it wouldn't be taken away from them.

I love cookies, peanut butter, and cereal. A little bit of each is ok. But I generally would consume them to the detriment of my health.

Even reading a book can go both ways for me. Getting into a book is almost like getting on an airplane. I am transported to an alternate reality. Reading can be a great way to escape from a current reality that is unpleasant. I have been known to stay up all night to devour a book.

What do you love that you think could be both good and bad for you? How do you deal with that?

60

Education is the passport to the future, for tomorrow belongs to those who prepare for it today. — Malcolm X

I am a lifelong learner. An education has definitely taken me around the world. I learned to read early and taught my children to read early. I started traveling at a young age and took my children on that journey at young ages. Learning another language and learning accounting and math were like learning the language of numbers. Learning different modes of dance and yoga was learning the language of the body. The culmination of all of these languages have prepared me for life now. I'm a linguist who is fluid in more than verbal languages, monetary languages, and body languages. I have learned to listen to what is said and what isn't said.

My grandmother raised a family and worked over 30 years in healthcare services and left her husband and moved from the U.S. Virgin Islands to New York City with no more than an eighth-grade education. She did not have as much book knowledge as some, but she was educated and did prepare. I was the person who wrote checks and read letters. Most people, even if they're illiterate, are highly functional and even experts in other ways. There are many musicians that cannot read music or singers that cannot read. My grandmother was the master of her domain.

How has your education or lack of education made you prepare? Who can you appreciate for their tenacity and their ways and their abilities of functioning, even if they are not considered literate? How can your education (life experience or books) make you happy?

61

The rule in the art world is: you cater to the masses or you kowtow to the elite; you can't have both. — Ben Hecht

This is fascinating and I really want to have a whole conversation about this. My oldest son is an artist. He doesn't fit in either one of these categories; his art has always come from him. Even when he was in elementary school when he was "discovered" and his art teacher took his artwork to school with him (he was in a PhD program at Columbia University). The teacher was so excited to tell me the he could get Sule into an art program for children with the MoMA. Sule wasn't interested. I clearly remember my son telling me, "Mom, they're going to make me draw pictures of flowers and vases...and I do monsters." He is still that person today. He has developed international notoriety by painting his heart, his emotions, and his characters. I don't think they look like monsters anymore, but you'll have to look up his art for yourself. He does characters that are big black men. And with the state of the world today —

wherever you stand with racial and economic politics — they might be monsters to someone. I really do have to have this conversation with him, but I digress.

That quote seems so cynical; there is some part of having it all. Only you get to define what "having it all" means. We write the script. Having it all to me means that I make enough to do the things that I want, spend time with people I love, travel to the places I want to go, support various philanthropic efforts, and pay my bills on time. I don't have a six-figure salary as of the time of this writing. I did before, so other people thought I had it all. I did not. And now by U.S. and capitalist standards I probably don't have it all, but by my definition I do.

What does "having it all" mean to you?

62

Advice is like snow — the softer it falls, the longer it dwells upon, and the deeper it sinks into the mind.
— Samuel Taylor Coleridge

This could be a parenting quote. The things that I said over and over to my children were like jingles and phrases. It's quite interesting to hear myself ask the question, "What did I say?" — and hear my adult children answer what I said to them in their preteen years.

You communicate deeply, and how you deliver the message is just as important as the actual message. As a native New Yorker, I've actually always loved riding the trains. It was fascinating to me to sit in a subway car and look at all these other humans and try to imagine what all of their stories were. The fact that some people are so passionate in their relationship to God that they stand in a subway car and proselytize has always been fascinating to me. They strategically pick a time when the train will be underground the longest. And at some point, you can't leave to go from one subway car to another. The subway car preachers yell to make sure you can hear them as we rumble under the streets of New York, moving from one part of the city to another. They tell you about the value of God and the things you need to do to be right in the eyes of God. I'm not going to discuss my spirituality and I'm not even discussing what's right or wrong, but what I will say is their method of yelling at the top of their lungs and invading someone else's private mental space might not be the best way to deliver their heartfelt, passionate message. Don't get me wrong; I have a deep abiding respect for how passionate they are and how important saving me is to them. But I can't hear people when they're yelling at the top of their lungs. That message of screaming and crying only works when there is danger or an infant involved.

How effective are you at delivering your messages? Have you noticed that if you say something and leave it alone, then say it again later and leave it alone, that it settles into someone's mind better? What seems to work? What doesn't work? What can you improve to invite ease and joy for all parties involved?

63

We cannot create what we can't imagine.
— Lucille Clifton

It is fascinating to think of the pyramids in Egypt. There were builders who were able to think of and create things beyond our imagination. I feel like that when I watch television, when I see a movie, and when I see someone dance. It's not just the dancer; that dance came from the mind of a choreographer. It's not just the musician, but that sound was put together by someone; it came from their mind, their vision, and their creation. When I look at art (where someone created a concept and their vision of something) it is breathtaking for me. And then I look at myself and how I've tended to limit what I do by a lack of imagination. It's not as though anyone put limits on me. I think about times I've been told I was too big, too short, or too something else to do something I wanted to do. Also, I don't always like being in the front of things. Sometimes it's ok, but other times it's not. I created a story in my mind that if I did all the things I love to do and was the fabulous theatrical performer I wanted to be, I would have to sacrifice my privacy and the quality of my life. So, I opted to create art within boundaries of what I deem to be safe. I limited my growth, because I thought it wouldn't be safe if I was too famous.

How have you limited yourself based on what you can't imagine or what you refuse to imagine?

64

There but for the grace of God go I.
— John Bradford

As a native New Yorker, I have grown accustomed to seeing homelessness and some of the worst representations of people with mental health challenges who aren't cared for properly. And I've had one experience in my life in which I was so sick, I could see myself as that person.

I was at home on my couch trapped in my body, I couldn't seem to control my speech (which was severely slurred), and my eyes rolled around in my head. Fortunately, two friends helped take care of me. As I write this, I can't even recall the name of what I had; I'm going to have to reach out to those friends and see if they remember. I don't have the same general practitioner anymore, so I can't even ask them. When things were back to "normal" and I could get on the train to go back to my management position in financial services, I saw someone with their head rolling around and talking to people I couldn't see. I wondered if they didn't have the ability or a community to care for whatever was ailing them and the situation got out of control. I wondered if that could have been me. Because it was scary for my friends and children to see what was happening to me those days on the couch.

I remain so grateful, so thankful for all that I have and all that I've had. Yes, some things were more challenging than others. Some things have been so challenging, I wouldn't wish them on anyone. But I do know that something could trigger a breakdown in me or anybody else. So, I don't judge as often or as harshly as I used to.

What situation can you allow more compassion for if you consider that you could possibly be in that situation?

65

Doubt kills more dreams than failure ever will. — Suzy Kassem

---

If doubt can kill dreams, it definitely kills joy! Are you ok with accepting some of the unknown? What I've learned about myself and my children is this absolute desire to know something — as in being 100% clear — keeps people from moving forward. Then you feel stuck, so you have a vision being stuck in quicksand and just sinking deeper and deeper. Sometimes, accepting that you cannot know everything can be freeing. I call this stuck place "analysis paralysis." Steven Pressfield called it resistance in his book, *The War of Art*. With most of my clients, doubt gets them stuck; they feel they don't know enough to take action.

If you can accept and create parameters that include the unknown, there is less doubt and then you can move forward.

Let's go with the example of me writing a book. I've

been writing for years. I have lots of journals. I've written articles and blogs, but I didn't see myself as a writer. So, the doubt about what to write, how to write, and being hyper critical made me not start writing a book. I questioned my message and if I was good enough to speak to you. Should I be writing? Can I be writing? Who will read what I write? All of those doubts kept me from doing it. I'm a writer, because the action of writing makes me so — and because you're reading this, I'm a published writer, an author.

Write down 2 or more things that you would do if you had no doubts. What fears or doubts keep you from trying? Pick one thing on your list; push "should" aside and do it!

I've learned that people will forget what you said, people will forget what you did, but people will never forget how you made them feel. — Maya Angelou

---

Are you aware of how you make people feel? If you're not sure, think of the people that you enjoy being around; think of how they make you feel. Ask a few people what impact you leave on them. If it's something you like, great; if it's something you don't like, you can change it. Create your legacy by looking at how you shift other people's energy. Learn from them, how you make them feel. During life in the pandemic, I learned that people valued my messages, beliefs, and Dionne-isms enough to seek them out. I learned how I made people feel because they sought me out on social media. It was a bit overwhelming. I realized I had underestimated the value that my presence brought to spaces and people. Honestly, it was heartwarming and overwhelming in equal measure. My students quoted me and remembered me, my quotes and my stories. I made them happy; they felt better about themselves and their lives. They felt hopeful. Wow. Goal accomplished.

What do people feel or remember about you that leaves an impact on them? If it is not in alignment with what you want it to be, change it.

67

Real change, enduring change, happens one step at a time. — Ruth Bader Ginsburg

---

The thing about change happening one step at a time is you have to walk a mile before you can see it has occurred. You don't need to see the end goal, just appreciate each one of the steps you take. Every step you take is a success.

Put one foot in front of the other. Do so literally by walking for physical and mental health. Do so figuratively by taking steps toward your goals. Do you remember the 1993 movie *Groundhog Day*, with Bill Murray? He hated that he kept living the same day over and over again. Then he shifted his perspective and learned so many things by practicing a little each day. He mastered playing the piano, sculpting ice, and even speaking French. He became a better person one day, one step, one lesson at a time.

What change are you striving to make? What step can you take today towards that change?

68

We need to reshape our own perception of how we view ourselves. We have to step up as women and take the lead.
— Beyoncé Knowles

This quote is not only for women, but I definitely see how in so many areas, countries, and places women are undervalued. But that first part about shaping the perception of how we see ourselves is crucial. The thoughts you feed yourself about yourself impact your reality. Regardless of your gender, how can you see yourself in a better life and step into that?

If you're seeing yourself as a failure, that's what you're living in the world. If you perceive yourself as successful and happy, you can create that ripple in the universe and step into that. There are more actions that will need to be taken. I have oversimplified it here, but those simplified steps are a part of what gets you in action to be a better you.

How do you see yourself? Pick one thing to improve and start working today to shift your perception.

69

You can imprison a man, but not an idea. You can exile a man, but not an idea. You can kill a man, but not an idea.
— Benazir Bhutto

Even though this is a gender binary quote, it immediately brings one woman to mind, Roberta Siegel. There's no history about her other than in the lives of all the people whose heart she touched. Roberta Siegel was my fourth-grade elementary school teacher. She was a white female, divorced, lived alone, and taught children in the South Bronx. She was gifted as a teacher. I learned so much from her. It's an honor at 54 years of age to talk about how significant her role in my life was and the ideas she planted in me.

In the 1970s, New York City public schools were extremely overcrowded. But Miss Siegel figured out a way to split the class into two groups, so she could work with us the best way possible. And because we were at different levels, she would simply write the assignments on the blackboard. So, we worked at our own pace. If you finished before the other students, you had the opportunity to help someone else with their work or move on to another assignment. I generally helped someone else and moved on to the next assignment.

I lived in the Millbrook Projects in the South Bronx, New York City. Miss Siegel realized that so many of us had not been exposed to other communities, ways of being, and even places just outside of our respective neighborhoods. But I had traveled by airplane to St. Thomas, U.S. Virgin Islands to visit my family. I had also visited family in Brooklyn and Queens, and some people I knew had their own cars and houses. This might not sound like a lot, but it was a lot for me especially when compared to other people living in the projects (government-subsidized housing).

Another idea Miss Siegel instilled in me was that I did not have to be a wife or a mother. Again, maybe this was not monumental. But for this little girl in 1975, when everybody in my family had children, it was. Some of them did not have husbands, but had multiple children. Therefore, it was a foregone conclusion to me that your life was complete as a mother; possibly as a wife, but definitely as a mother. Miss Siegel was not only someone who consciously decided not to have children (because she did not want children) — but also she had been married and had opted to get a divorce.

I had only heard of women being left by men or men choosing not to marry the women with whom they had children. Before Roberta Siegel, I did not know anything about the concept of a woman choosing to get a divorce or choosing not to have children.

What idea has been planted in your mind (consciously or unconsciously) and what do you remember about it?

70

Do the best you can until you know better. Then when you know better, do better.
— Maya Angelou

Are you doing your best? No judgment. This is purely an inquiry; I'm being curious. You can ask yourself how you're doing. What can you learn from that inquiry? I've learned many tools that help me focus my energy, my time, and ways to plan, so I can get out of my way. I have found that if I'm not learning, I am not doing my best. As a result of being curious and learning, I move forward. Sometimes, that inquiry I just mentioned puts me in action to do better and to do more.

Sometimes we judge our past based on our present knowledge. We punish ourselves for not doing better when we did not know what we know now.

People have often asked me about how I got over my guilt after my daughter died by suicide. But there was no guilt. I was also asked how I could care for her father

---

after his spinal injury and do I regret it. I did what I felt was the right thing in each situation. Perhaps with what I know now things would be different. But I do not go down that proverbial rabbit hole. I did the best I could with the information I had at that time, for each situation.

Your best changes each day. Are you doing your best today? What could you do better with more knowledge? How will you get that knowledge?

71

The best time to plant a tree was 20 years ago. The second best time is now.
— Chinese proverb

Get in action. Sometimes, we spend so much time talking about what we should have done, what we could have done, and what we wish we had done — but it's not too late! That thing can be done now. Of course, sometimes this is related to something or someone that might no longer be around.

Perhaps you wanted to say something to someone who is no longer alive. You can still talk to your loved ones after they're gone. That's been a realization that has brought me great peace around all of my loved ones who've died over the years. I talk to them and sometimes hear answers in nature. Bring closure to what you cannot do in the way you once wanted to do and do what can be done now. Say the things. Write the letters. Edit the list. Make a decision to do it or not do it.

Action is the cure. What is one thing on your bucket list or your to-do list that's been on your mind for too long? What is one step you can take towards completing it today?

72

Never put off till tomorrow what you can do today. — Thomas Jefferson

Well, that is totally easier said than done, right? The topic of procrastination could be an entire book. There are seminar leaders who make their living teaching people how to do things and how to be in action; basically, how not to procrastinate.

There are so many emotional reasons to put things off. There are physical reasons as well. But it's hard to deny the feeling of success once we complete the tasks that have been put off. Stepping into the new space of, "It is done." I'm confident that's how I'll feel when this book is completed. There has been a level of not wanting to see, feel, or remember certain things, so it was an emotional process for me and a time process. Perhaps think about procrastination in a different way; focus on the joy that completing something will bring you and see if that propels you into action.

I am a master procrastinator. Often busy doing something that is not the most important thing to do when I am doing it. I recruit people to support me in my vision so I can complete things. I will even use social media to declare what I am doing to get support. I might not be willing to be in action for myself but I will do it so I can keep my word. My students know that I will often tell them I am going to do something, so I actually do it. Accountability partners are awesome. If your friend or family are not willing perhaps you can find a group on social media. Social media is not bad in managed doses. Sometime a group of us on Facebook will hold each other accountable for our workouts and our water intake.

Accountability kills procrastination. Make a list of people that will hold you accountable to your plan. Tell them one or two things you plan to complete by a certain date. Write out the steps AND all of the emotions and resistance that come up to stop you.

73

Without a struggle, there can be no progress. — Frederick Douglass

If you're reading this book, at some point you were born and there are many ways to have been born; it could've been a vaginal ("natural") birth or a C-section. The process of birth is a struggle. A life form was created by a union of two people. This being grows and gets really comfortable for about nine months. Then he or she gets pushed through a canal that seems so small in comparison, it defies all logic for this being to come out and take up space in this world. That is the first lesson we get about struggle. Whether we deem ourselves ready or have a consciousness that understands what's happening at a certain point in time, we get pushed out into the world. This might not be what you thought of when you read that quote, but I love looking at the expansion of things. This is a lesson we've been getting since we were born, and you may not have made that association.

Struggle is a natural part of life and we can decide how we feel about it. It doesn't have to make us sad or angry; it can possibly bring us joy. We get to choose how we feel about something.

Pick a past or present struggle and decide how you feel about it. Practice detached awareness when you write about the struggle and about the feelings.

74

**Power concedes nothing without a demand. It never did and it never will.
— Frederick Douglass**

I feel when he said this, it was about freedom for Africans in the United States during the times of slavery — since he was an abolitionist. That was a major external battle. But even now we sometimes have fights that are internal with ourselves and it is a power struggle. It may not be a fight with someone outside of yourself; it may be a fight with some aspect of yourself internally. That is one of the power struggles I think I engage in the most, me fighting with myself. I am the one who has to demand that I'm taking control of a situation and choosing joy over pain, happiness over sadness, and sleep over work.

Whether it's an internal or external battle, what can you choose to have power over today that will bring you closer to your joy?

75

There is no royal flower strewn path to success. And if there is, I have not found it, for whatever success I have attained has been the result of much hard work and many sleepless nights.
— Madam C. J. Walker

During the year I was writing this book, Madam C.J. Walker was like a spirit animal or a guardian angel for me. I remember watching the four-part Netflix series about her life, wanting to know more about her, really appreciating the effort she put into her process, and respecting the all the sacrifices she made. Madam C. J. Walker gave up her family; she didn't give birth to children (she adopted them) and her marriage failed. She did so many things "right" and just as many things "wrong."

But the level of sacrifice she made gave her a certain level of pride and joy. Madam C. J. Walker didn't spend a lot of time questioning whether her dreams and methods were valid. She kept forging ahead, reinventing herself, and creating new methods when things got in her way.

Be that curious about your joy and how to get there. Maybe you don't need to create a new project and find a new way to make it a sensation in your country. Perhaps the new legacy you're leaving is a way to be happy in your body and life. That could be the example you set for yourself and your peers. I hope to create a movement as a contagion in the world, so we can be at peace personally and collectively.

How can you keep forging ahead and reinventing yourself in spite of obstacles?

76

If you want to go fast, go alone. If you want to go far, go together.
– African proverb

Almost everything I have achieved, that I am proud of, I have had support. I gained 80 lbs. on my own. But, when I wanted to lose 80 lbs., I set my goals 5 lbs. at a time, and told everyone. When I wanted to go to Africa it started with getting my passport and finding a group to go with. When I wanted to buy my house, I made sure I had good credit. When I decide to reach for the heavens and I'm really clear on it being a massive goal, I build support. When I decided that I would take 365 yoga classes in 365 days I told everybody. I posted it on social media and people supported my effort. They would come to class with me or motivate me when I was tired. When people run full marathons there are cheering sections. When I decided to participate in my first Overnight walk in 2013, I posted it on Facebook. My friend in VA asked me who was going with me and she decided to support me. (Thanks Nana!)

You are not alone. There are people that you know, and some that you do not know, that are willing to support your dream and goals if only they knew what they were.

Pick 1-2 big goals. Break those big goals into baby steps and get (physical or virtual) support.

77

If you have to let go and begin again thousands of times, that's fine. That's the practice. — Sharon Salzburg

---

I have been in the process of reinventing myself for longer than I can recall. Starting. Stopping. Giving up. Starting again. Hell, that was even my college graduation story. I graduated from high school young with all the promise in the world of what I would do. I went off to college at 16, but then didn't graduate until I was 20-something. I went back to college a second time — but then I had my son and couldn't finish college as planned. I did go back a third time to finish the last six credits (two classes). So, nothing about my journey has been start at Point A, go to Point B, get to Point Z, and then finish. My journey through life has been like the "Family Circus" cartoon strip or Pablo Coelho's *The Alchemist*. There have been lots of starts and stops along the way and lots of learning.

What story do you have about your journey? What steps can you make to finish something? What decisions can you make about something that should no longer be finished?

78

There is only one way to eat an elephant, one bite at a time. — Desmond Tutu

I truly cannot think of a task in my life that didn't seem like it was too much for me. I went to first grade at five years old. I skipped eighth grade. I graduated from high school at 16. I went straight to college. I dropped out. I went back. I almost graduated, but then got pregnant. I went back and earned my degree. My family lived in the South Bronx. I was on public assistance as a child and as an adult. I made less than $40,000 a year in New York City as a single parent, but I eventually bought a house in Manhattan. Just take one bite at a time.

What feels like too much for you right now? What's the bite that you can take today?

79

God only gives you what you can handle.
— Author Unknown

I spent a lot of years wondering where the Appeals Board was. I'm a person who is about processes. I felt I had been given more than I could handle, and I didn't know who to take that up with. I'm of the generation where I know I can lose, but I also know I can fight. And if I disagree with a particular decision there's a process where I can say, "I don't agree with this. How can we fix it?" But I couldn't figure out where the Appeals Board was and how to deal with it.

So, I figured out what I could do for myself. I would appeal MY decision. I would appeal belief that the horrible thing I had endured was the end of me. I appealed to my inner wisdom and that of my friends, family, and ancestors. I decided that there was possibility and hope at the end of the despair I was currently feeling. Whether it was being in the hospital with nephritis; in the hospital with a severe case of pneumonia that had yet to be diagnosed; at home healing from irritable bowel syndrome and looking, speaking, and feeling like I was insane. Being so full of fecal matter, the waste in my colon had tilted my pelvis and thrown my back out. The weight gain. The physical abuse. The emotional abuse. The sexual harassment. The attempted rape. The rape.

Why did God think I could handle all of those things?! I still don't know. But I'm really happy that I lived to tell the story and I found joy on the other side of pain.

What can you decide that could make a difference in your current perception of someone (even yourself) or a situation?

80

This too shall pass. — Author Unknown

I cannot tell you how much I dislike this quote. Especially as a youth, it always felt like an "old" person's way of saying give it time. I was so over time healing all wounds. And I can't say I like the quote now, but I'm far more forgiving of it than I was in my twenties. It does seem that things do pass. But when someone is suffering, this quote just doesn't feel helpful to me.

It's important to know yourself, to know what will take you down the proverbial rabbit hole and what will help you climb out of the rabbit hole. I have learned to take a deep breath when someone says this to me. I remind myself that they sincerely mean well and I receive it as a loving thought meant to sooth my spirit.

Reflect on how your responses to certain comments have changed over time. Write about your healthy responses to triggers.

81

She made broken look beautiful and strong look invincible. She walked with the universe on her shoulders and made them look like a pair of wings. — Ariana

---

In extreme periods of stress, I often receive the compliment that I look good. I close my mouth and I keep squeezing everything in on the inside and compressing it. Other yoga teachers look at me and say, "Your skin is so beautiful; you look so calm." And I stare back at them in disbelief, trying to process how I can literally feel like I'm dying on the inside and they're experiencing a very different perception of me.

Generally, I don't see what other people see when they look at me. I don't know who does. But I have come to believe that my body has created a process of taking the external pressure from the world. When it comes into my body, I pull it in; it becomes a magnet that pulls all the negativity into one place, and then I work on releasing that. Sometimes I succeed, and sometimes I

---

don't. I would dare say in the times that I did not succeed, I wound up being extremely ill and sometimes hospitalized. One time I was in the hospital and they couldn't figure out what was wrong at first. Later, they diagnosed me with pneumonia. I look back at the pictures and am amazed that I was in a hospital bed, but I appeared healthy from the outside.

This quote is important because we all need to acknowledge that someone's outward appearance is not always an accurate reflection of what's happening on the inside. You are not alone, and you don't have to make broken look beautiful.

Who are your "strong" friends? Contact one of them today and see how they are. Reflect on your mood today, on a scale of 1 - 10, how are you? Tell someone your rating. Get help if you are at or below the number 6.

82

Caring for myself is not self-indulgence, it is self-preservation, and that is an act of political warfare. — Audre Lorde

---

Over the years, I've become a master at self-care. I don't think I was always this way. But even in intensely busy times of work, I make time to go for a walk, meditate, take a shower, or sleep. Sometimes, I take a bath, schedule a facial or a colonic, or take myself out to eat. You don't have to spend money. You could have a mini-facial in your house; it could be something as simple as honey on your face. I'm really big into skin care and massage. I give a lot and work my body to the max. So, it's important for me to give back to my body so it will continue to work for me. And I definitely have received negative comments at times about the things I do for myself or the money I spend to do those things. But that's my business. How you choose to take care of yourself is your business and it's important, because you are important.

What will you do or schedule today to help you take care of you? What does self-care look like for you?

83

A woman's ability to make everyone in the room feel at home should never be construed as weakness. — Benazir Bhutto

Sometimes, power is misrepresented by loudness and pressure — but if we look at nature, water is always powerful. It's not only powerful when it's a wave, a blizzard, or a tsunami. It's always powerful. Air is always powerful, even if it's not a tornado or hurricane. When a woman makes people feel comfortable and at home, it's like still water. There's a sense of calm, even with waterfalls. So, a woman is not weak by making someone feel comfortable; she's like still water and still very much a force of nature.

How can you embrace your power? How can you redefine what others may consider weakness?

84

Yoga is a journey from self, to self, through self. — #dionnesays

It's amazing to see yourself in three different places: past, present, and future. I spend a lot of time in reflection on that as well as layers of time, layers of me, and layers of life. I love how I've paraphrased this quote to make it real for myself and my students.

Step on your mat. Start to create a vision of what you're creating and how you're creating it, as you move towards yourself. The breathing, the stillness, the fastness, or the slowness all make a difference on how you approach you. Surrender, release, death, birth and triumph all exist on the mat. On or off a yoga mat, time travel is possible.

Whether you have a yoga practice or not, do the following. Speak to a younger version of yourself and let them know how you are doing. Ask your future self for advice. Write about what comes up for you.

85

Our deepest fear is not that we are inadequate. Our deepest fear is that we are powerful beyond measure. It is our light, not our darkness that most frightens us. We ask ourselves, who am I to be brilliant, gorgeous, talented, fabulous? Actually, who are you not to be? — Marianne Williamson

The fear of success is what this ultimately discusses. And if living a life filled with joy is what you're afraid of, how do we remove that fear? So many people are willing to do for others what they might not do for themselves, so step into being your most fabulous self for your future self. I've often had lots of conversations with myself, as in Dionne talking to Dionne. I would tell my students, "Don't worry, Dionne gets on my nerves too." When they made a strange face, I would say, "Yes, I'm talking about me."

So, to motivate myself I often talk to myself as my best friend. Spoiler alert: you are your best friend. When there is nobody else around, you are there. So, develop that love relationship with yourself. I would tell Dionne that she was going to get through it, and she'd be fine; just take one little step and over time each little step would move forward. That moved me forward and ultimately moved us forward. I'm very much a community or village person. So, when I learn something exciting, I bring that information to my community and try to move people forward with me.

If you don't want to share your greatness for yourself, share it for your future self, for people you like, love, or want to inspire. If the only motivation you have is your future self, use that. See your future self, name your future self, and aspire to take the steps needed to become that future self.

How does this quote resonate with you? Write about your fears. Who or what situation made you decide to shrink? Why did you decide not to be great?

86

If you can't love yourself, how you gonna love anybody else? — RuPaul Charles

We often say that we want people to love us. One of the major laments in global society is the desire for a single person to be in a partnership with another person, an intimate relationship. Perhaps even a legal commitment or marriage. But some of the same people do not have a loving relationship with themselves.

People lament and doubt their worthiness and beauty. They look in the mirror and are disgusted by what they see but want someone to love them. Recently a client said to me she was sad or angry in the morning. We went deeper and she hated waking up alone and that was a trigger for her feeling like she will always wake up alone and would never have a life partner or children. Another client is okay with being single but does not like her body.

My stretch marks are badges of honor. I earned most

of them from carrying children. I also earned some from being over 200 lbs. I did not like being a size 2x on my 5'0" frame but gave myself grace and time to change what no longer served me. I love myself and forgave myself for eating my emotions, sadness, anger and stress.

Thank your body today. Thank your breath, eyes, ears, nose, teeth, hair, stretch marks, thank ALL of the physical you. As you bathe or moisturize say, BODY BEAUTI-FUL. Let that be your mantra as often as you remember. Give yourself compliments and learn to receive them from other people.

Write down at least 10 positive things about yourself. If you cannot come up with any, ask a friend or family member.

87

Do you want to meet the love of your life? Take a look in the mirror. — Byron Katie

You are stuck with yourself for the rest of your life. And if you are fortunate, that will be a long time. So, establishing an intimate, loving, and engaged relationship with yourself is important. Also, you teach other people how to treat you based on how you treat yourself. So, start loving up on yourself. Love up on yourself so much that someone else will see what you see in the mirror and want to get to know you. And you will know how to love someone else, because you love yourself. That other person will know how to love you, because you've modeled love so well. Loving yourself is one of many paths to joy and happiness.

Look into your eyes and say, "I love you." Write, "I love you" and at least 5 other affirmations down. As often as possible, say these affirmations out loud to yourself in front of a mirror.

88

Find a job you enjoy doing, and you will never have to work a day in your life.
— Mark Twain

I grew up with my mother and grandmother watching soap operas, *All My Children, One Life to Live, As the World Turns, The Young and the Restless*, et cetera. I recall people planning their schedule around what was coming on TV. This was before you could record TV shows or see them on demand. But someone that loved watching soap operas had the great idea to do a summary! Soap Opera Digest was a big deal in the 1970s!

Do you know what you love? Take a few moments each day and reflect on things that make you happy. Cooking, writing, reading, watching TV, watching movies, talking to people, answering questions, researching, drawing, music, technology, playing video games, and dancing. There is some way of making money from what you love and there's somebody who's done it already, but they didn't do it like you. Only you can do it like you.

What do you love doing that people will pay for?

**God, give me grace to accept with serenity
the things that cannot be changed,
Courage to change the things
which should be changed,
and the wisdom to distinguish
the one from the other.**

**Living one day at a time,
Enjoying one moment at a time,
Accepting hardship as a pathway to
peace...
— Reinhold Niebuhr**

My grandmother LOVED the Serenity Prayer. It was around the house in several forms. A plate (now hanging on my wall). A candle molded in the shape of praying hands that was always on the dining table. Written beautifully and framed on the wall.

Not until I searched the internet did I learn there was another verse. That last line strikes home for me, "Accepting hardship as a pathway to peace."

It makes so much sense. Bad things are going to happen, so it's important that we learn to shift our perspective. If we can look at these things as a pathway to peace, that creates a different ability to deal with it and embrace it. I don't know if I'll ever get to the point that I'll be happy about a challenge, but I do feel a lot better with the perception of it being a pathway to peace.

Tell a different story about a particularly challenging situation. Focus on your growth from the hardship so you can move towards joy and peace in your life. Write the new story here. Read it out loud to yourself or someone else.

90

Children learn more from what you are than what you teach. — W.E.B. Dubois

Growing up, I often heard adults say, "Do as I say, not as I do." In my observation, this sets children up for failure. We are all consistently watching what people around us are doing. So, we get this mixed message and start to make decisions about this person. For example. I love and respect this person and I want to emulate this person. But they just told me not to do what they do. So, I should listen to their words but not monitor their actions? This is a lesson not only for children. We are all teaching someone how to behave and how to treat us.

Do you model the behaviors you would like others to emulate? Are you happy with the behaviors you show to others? If you are, I applaud you. If you're not, how can you change that?

91

Planning is the way to let the universe know what you want. — Monica Shah

Success requires planning. — #dionnesays

Write it down. Whether you're using pen or paper, if it's electronic get it out of your head and into the world. Whether you're working on your physical body, your life, your friends, or your family, get it out of your head; make a plan. If you don't think you can do it on your own, make a plan and share it with somebody. Have an accountability partner. Success requires planning. The universe wants to support you, your dreams, and your ideas, but you have to tell it what to do. When you get clear, the universe will get clear as well.

And if you're not sure what it is yet, just keep writing and writing. It doesn't have to be pen and paper. It could be dictating, transcribing, or typing — but get it out of your head, so you can create it in the real world, step into it, and shape it.

I apparently have always been a planner. I would plan how I was spending my money and balance my wallet (yes wallet not checkbook) each day. My mother would chuckle as she told people that I would actually plan a nap into my busy day. #successrequiresplanning

If you want to transform your health you will need to plan your food, your water, your exercise. If you are starting or growing a business you will need a business plan. #successrequiresplanning

Write down something you want to do, and list the steps you need to take to accomplish that thing. Pick a completion date and enlist support. Write down the distractions and fears as they come up.

92

Dance like nobody's watching; love like you've never been hurt. Sing like nobody's listening; live like it's heaven on earth.
— Mark Twain

I am a dancer at my core. Maybe you are a dancer at your core too. I've got a food dance when my meal is yummy. I've got a happy dance. Then I dance when there's music that touches my soul or brings up a memory. There's a way that I dance to music and there's a way that I dance through life.

If you're reading this, you've probably been hurt before. I know I kissed and married a few frogs, and they did not become princes. Many people have tried a multitude of intimate relationships before they found the "right one." Many people have been hurt a lot before they found peace and partnership with another human. Maybe you are happily single or maybe you are happy in love.

Maybe you only sing in the shower or maybe you have

a career in singing. Regardless of how you dance, love, sing or live, there is a certain freedom to moving through your life without fear of being judged.

In vivid detail, write down what you would do and how would you live without fear of judgment? Where would you live? How would you look? Would you be in a relationship? What would your job be? Periodically read this vision out loud to yourself or someone else.

93

You've got to learn to leave the table when love is no longer being served.
— Nina Simone

Sometimes, we make decisions that are not in our best interest. Long before I got married, I decided I wasn't going to get a divorce. I felt there were too many divorces in my family, and I wasn't going to fall into that statistic. I think I issued a challenge to the universe and it accepted. I married a man and withstood a lot more emotional and mental abuse than I ever should have before I decided to get up from the table, because love was no longer being served. And quite honestly it really was never being served, but I couldn't see that while I was in it. It took me going through a few years and several challenges in that marriage to stand up for myself and walk away.

Maya Angelou said, "When people show you who they are believe them *the first time*." Paul did tell me who he was before we got married and I listened with my heart and didn't hear what he was saying. So, I honestly believe that divorce was on me because he told me who and how he was. He told me how he treated women and he did not *want* to do that to me. That was January 1995. I heard that he knew his faults and was working on them. But that was not what he said. I could not fathom that someone knew how harsh they were and wasn't working to fix that. I. Was. WRONG. I learned.

Do you listen with your ears, your eyes, or your heart? How has that served you? What have you learned?

94

When they go low, we go high.
— Michelle Obama

Paul and I were still legally married longer than we should have been. I had paid for the marriage and I refused to pay for the divorce. We had separate lives and he was on my health insurance. On a Friday before Palm Sunday, I got a call that he had a spinal injury. He was in Jamaica; St. Ann's, if my memory serves me correctly. Paul was a fitness model on a shoot. He had a spinal injury on a trampoline. Ruptured his vertebrae, C4-C5. It was almost like the Christopher Reeve accident. Paul was paralyzed from the neck down. I asked the doctor in Jamaica what he would do if it was his child and he said he would have him flown back to the United States.

Because was a Friday on a holiday weekend, I could not get insurance approval to have an air ambulance fly Paul to New York City. I called my dentist, as her husband was a surgeon. She recommended Lenox Hill Hospital and suggested a doctor. I had to charge $19,000 on

---

three different credit cards to get Paul back to New York City. After that was paid for, I had to call his parents and explain to my elementary school-aged children what had happened. Oh, and this was on Paul's birthday. And my son's birthday party was scheduled for Palm Sunday. Paul underwent a 10-hour surgery to remove the shrapnel of his crushed vertebrae from his neck. A rod, titanium perhaps, was put into his neck.

We had my son's birthday party in the park. There were kids, parents, pizza, a movie, and cupcakes. Once the kids were in bed, I went back to Lenox Hill Hospital. I was there daily and spoke with many doctors and nurses. I finally turned Paul over to his family. When he got out of the hospital, he was moved to rehab. He had to learn to walk and use his hands again.

I got the money back. The insurance was approved. I paid all the credit card bills. Paul's mother and sister brought him home to what was our apartment when we lived together as a family. When Paul got home and our daughter wanted to see him, he told me, "It was not a good time."

Despite all of the abuse, I had to do what I felt was right. I had to be able to live with myself. I would do it again even now, because at that time I did what I felt was right for my daughter's father. He had consistently gone low. And life gave me the opportunity to walk my talk. I believe I always went high.

Life will challenge you to be who you say you are. Be clear in your values. How do you "walk your talk?" How can you create joy in spite of life's downs?

95

There is always light, if only we're brave enough to see it. If only we're brave enough to be it. —Amanda Gorman

It's wonderful to collect quotes from history, but it's also wonderful to have been alive to hear and remember when they were said. Watching the 2021 presidential inauguration was special for a number of reasons. At the time this book was written, Amanda Gorman's book hadn't been released yet — but it was already sold out before it was released and I'm sure there are many more quotes to come, but this is the one that struck the world. It was a pivotal part of history.

During my darkest times, I was committed to my light and my joy and not allowing anyone to dim my light. I was in an abusive relationship and started to have doubts about myself, my worth, and my possibilities. So, listening to this young woman read or speak such salient truths took me back to the pain and hardship I'd endured in order to come to that conclusion.

Are you the light? How can you be the light? What prevents you from being the light?

96

Bring your humanity to your art. Bring your art to humanity. — Maxime Lagacé

Your art, above and beyond anything you do outside of yourself, is YOU. How you dress, how you speak, how you do your hair, if you wear polish on your nails, if you wear jewelry, etc. How you show up is art. How you give yourself to humanity, shapes humanity.

Your fingerprint is unique to you. Even if you are an identical twin, your fingerprint is unique to you. You were designed.

YOU are a work of art.

Write this down. "I am unique. I am a work of art." List at least 10 things that define you, your personality and your sense of style. If you are stumped, ask your friends and family and they will tell you what they see.

97

A good laugh and a long sleep are the two best cures for anything. — Irish proverb

My daughter Siwe loved Kevin Hart. As a part of her coping strategies and mechanisms, she had some of his stuff on her iPod. When life gets you down and you can't find joy or laughter on your own, there is always comedy. Comedians play an important role in our lives as the people that make us laugh.

When you're stressed sleep might be difficult, but finding ways to take short naps and getting support, sleep, and laughter go a long way. For the most part, I sleep well. But when life gets in the way and I cannot sleep, I figure out some other strategies to help me sleep well. If you're dealing with insomnia, your sleep is troubled, or you're not getting enough sleep, it can impact your physical, mental and emotional health. If using a meditation or sleep app doesn't help, seek medical or emotional support.

Make a list of what makes you laugh.

Make a list of what helps you sleep.

Keep these lists handy when you need to refer to them. When your moods are off, check in with yourself to see if you are getting enough laughter or sleep.

98

A balanced diet is a cookie in each hand.
— Barbara Johnson

I grew up on *Sesame Street*. The Cookie Monster was my favorite character, because that was me. I'm not a baker or pastry chef. I am a cook. I think cookies should be on the food pyramid. In every country! As this quote says balance is important, but there's something special about food, love, and comfort. Everywhere in the world, there are certain dishes that are traditional. Plus, we need sweetness in our life. Have you heard of a bitter cookie? Some of the balance we desire in life is some assurance that things might not always be sweet, but there is a balance. With this quote, there is a light-hearted humorous reference to how many of us feel love and comfort from food.

Using your senses, write at least 10 ways you can create sweetness in your life. What can you touch, see, hear, smell, or taste that makes you happy?

99

Write it down on real paper, with a real pencil, and watch shit get real.
— Erykah Badu

There's something magical about writing something down. From my understanding, the Pharaohs during biblical times said, "So, let it be said. So, let it be written. So, let it be done."

I would often play this game with myself each year at Morgan Stanley. I would write down the amount of money that I thought I would make at the end of the year. At one point I was an hourly employee that was paid for overtime. I eventually became salaried and was no longer eligible for overtime, but I was eligible for year-end bonuses. I would write down an amount and put it away and forget about it. I would generally come within $1000 of my actual year-end pay.

Don't just think it, INK it. It's really important that we not only verbalize things, but also write them down. Somehow, bringing it from our mind and our body into the world is magical — even if it starts just with voice and paper, it's air and earth. Bring those elements to your vision, so then you can step into it and live your vision.

Write down a dream you've had in your head that you have not spoken about or written down? Look at it. Read it aloud periodically.

100

There is no force equal to a (wo)man determined to rise. — W.E.B. Dubois

However you identify, I would say that this holds true. Since I identify as a woman, I would like to say I do feel this force exists even more in women than in men. I think that is demonstrated in childbirth and stories of people having superhuman strength when there's an issue of safety for their loved ones or a child. I have read so many miraculous testimonials. Like Harriet Tubman walking hundreds of miles for her freedom and still committing to do that again and again for the possibility of bringing others to freedom.

What are you committed to and what do you need to get there? What obstacles are in your way? How can you work around them or remove them?

101

If this was all there was and there was no more, could you be happy? — #dionnesays

I have always had a way of checking in with myself to see if things were okay. I did have a bad temper and a sharp tongue as a child. I learned to take deep breaths to calm myself down before I spoke. I would often write out may anger as well. I also learned to sleep on something as well. If I woke up and that situation was still bothering me or if I couldn't sleep because of what was bothering me, I knew it needed to be addressed. Over time, I kept those things and added that question, "If this was all there was and there was no more, could you be happy?"

It was quite a helpful barometer to assess what my next steps should be. If the answer was a yes, no action required. But if the answer was a no, well action was required.

My first NYC apartment was not meant for a family. But

there we were, two adults and two children in an apartment that was barely 600 square feet. My ex-husband was often frustrated and unhappy. He made his disapproval clear, "I was too fat." "The apartment was too messy." "I did not clean up well enough."

I would ask myself that question, "If this was all there was and there was no more would I be happy?" And for the most part I kept answering yes. Even so, one day I did get a resounding NO.

When I got to the answer of no with my ex-husband, I started living at my mom's house until he could move out. Crazy times. Faking a happy marriage until the kids went to sleep and then going down the block to sleep at my mom's apartment and then coming home before the kids woke up. I was barely functioning at work and my boss could tell something was wrong. I thank her for calling me out. And getting me into therapy. He moved out, I became a single parent of two and the long road to healing began.

Write down anything that is getting in the way of your consistent joy. What are you willing to do to change that? Who can you tell? How can you enlist support where needed?

102

Bonus Quote

Even if it seems impossible, possible is always in the room. — Bethany Lyons

---

I was on my yoga mat when I heard Bethany say this. She was teaching a Baptiste Power Yoga class on the Lyons Den Digital platform. It was March 2021, one year into the global pandemic. The world was a mess. The USA was a mess and I was not in a good mental place. I needed to be on my mat regularly to get my head right.

We were in balancing half moon and she was challenging us all to try on something new. She suggested that we try a bind. So I reached my right hand back grabbed my right foot. She then suggested that we reach the other arm back and grab the foot with BOTH hands. Then she said, "Even if it seems impossible, possible is always in the room."

I did it. I had never done that before. I was in my house, on my mat, watching her and listening to her from my laptop. But I did it. Over 50, with arthritis and injuries, I

---

did it. Little things give me hope. I hope this book gave you hope.

She kept a small woman-owned business open in a global pandemic, transformed herself, and her business. She is a model for someone that makes the impossible, possible. I never told her about that. She is a mentor and a friend to many. She believed she could, and she did. She believed I could, and I did.

Who do you watch? Who do you admire? What do you learn form them? How can you make the impossible, possible?

AFFIRMATIONS

1. I love me.

2. I am whole.

3. I am happy.

4. I am one with the universe.

5. I am worthy.

6. I am loveable.

7. I accept help with grace.

8. I receive love with ease.

9. I am a glorious work-in-progress.

REFLECTIONS

_____

_____

_____

_____

_____

_____

_____

_____

_____

_____

_____

_____

_____

Joy is your birthright.

Transformation is possible.

Live Life INjoy!

AUTHOR'S NOTE

Thank you so much for reading through my words, thoughts, and processes. This has been a phenomenal journey for me and I am thankful that you are here. There are so many more stories to tell but this is just a bite size piece of life and I hope you chew it up and it's entirety and make changes. I invite you to live life INjoy. Joy is your birthright. Trust the process and at every step of the way even when things are challenging **Live Life INjoy!**

I would love to hear from you. If you have a story to share about your journey to please use the hashtag **#LiveLifeINjoy** or email me, dionne@joyousocean.com.

INjoy,

Dionne C. Monsanto
Chief Joy Connector
dionne@joyousocean.com

ABOUT THE AUTHOR

Dionne C. Monsanto, Chief Joy Connector and Founder of Joyous Ocean, connects people to their joy. As a life transformation coach, speaker, mental health advocate, and performer, she creates the space for her clients to safely realize their goals and build better versions of themselves.

Dionne's belief is that we can collectively change the world if we each build a joy-filled healthy body to support the lives we want to live. She believes that joy is your birthright and transformation is possible. In short, Dionne helps people Live Life INjoy! With her support, her clients create their "right-size" bodies and lives.

After leaving a successful financial services career, Dionne turned her passion for yoga, as well as her love of dance, into a budding six-figure business and has inspired and transformed communities and clients all over the world. The "Dionne effect" has reshaped bodies and lives in 6 of the 7 continents. She is a native New Yorker and a global citizen. As such she has been on TV, radio and in print; CBS News, Time Magazine, Essence, and more.

She currently holds a seat on the board of the NYC Chapter of the American Foundation for Suicide Prevention (AFSP) and sits on the National Chapter Leadership Council for AFSP as well. She is a serial helper who loves cooking, music, and laughter. She sees them all as moving meditations.

As a proud mother of three, she hopes to leave an example that her sons will follow so they can live happy, healthy lives and make her deceased daughter proud. On any given day, you will find Dionne with a coffee cup or water bottle in her hand while on her way to or from yoga, cooking, walking, or coaching. Dionne leads the way as the pied piper challenging us to claim joy as our birthright while calling us to live life INjoy.

Connect with Dionne on social media:
- Instagram **@DionneCMonsanto**
- LinkedIn **linkedin.com/in/DionneCMonsantoINjoy**
- Facebook **@DionneCMonsantoINjoy**
- Twitter **@JoyousOcean**

Learn more at **JoyousOcean.com**

A SPECIAL BONUS FROM dionne:
101 Ways to Live Life INjoy Journal

Thank you so much for reading **101 Ways to Live Life INjoy**. You have taken the first step to create your path to joy. You are on your way to connecting to both yourself and others in a spirit of growth, health, and compassion.

In the spirit of giving, I created this special bonus to add to your joy toolkit... ***The 101 Ways to Live Life INjoy Journal*** will help you capture your aha moments and reflections from the book so you can implement them faster and more easily. **#LifeLifeINjoy**

Just go to the link below and tell us where to send it.
JoyousOcean.com/journal

I'm rooting for you! I look forward to hearing about your breakdowns as well as your breakthroughs!

Here's to living life
INjoy,

Dionne C. Monsanto
Chief Joy Connector
dionne@joyousocean.com

Made in the USA
Middletown, DE
20 July 2022